THE FRENCH RENASCENCE

BY
CHARLES SAROLEA

KENNIKAT PRESS, INC./PORT WASHINGTON, N. Y.

THE FRENCH RENASCENCE

First published in 1916
Reissued in 1970 by Kennikat Press
Library of Congress Catalog Card No: 73-110920
SBN 8046-0902-0

Manufactured in the United States of America

CONTENTS

	PAGE
INTRODUCTION	9
MONTAIGNE	37
MONTAIGNE AND NIETZSCHE	49
PASCAL'S "THOUGHTS"	59
PASCAL AND NEWMAN	73
MADAME DE MAINTENON	89
LISELOTTE: A GERMAN PRINCESS AT THE COURT OF LOUIS XIV	111
SIR ARTHUR CONAN DOYLE ON THE FRENCH HUGUENOTS	137
ROUSSEAU'S "ÉMILE"	147
MARIE ANTOINETTE BEFORE THE REVOLUTION	155
MIRABEAU	167
ROBESPIERRE	179
THE REAL NAPOLEON	191
NAPOLEON AS A SOCIALIST	205
BALZAC	225
GUSTAVE FLAUBERT	239
MAURICE MAETERLINCK	249
THE CONDEMNATION OF MAETERLINCK	261
PROFESSOR BERGSON	271
MONS. POINCARÉ	285
THE NEW FRANCE	293

LIST OF ILLUSTRATIONS

	PAGE
MICHEL EYQUEM, SEIGNEUR DE MONTAIGNE	41
CHÂTEAU OF MONTAIGNE	45
JEAN JACQUES ROUSSEAU	149
HONORÉ GABRIEL RIQUETI MIRABEAU	173
HONORÉ DE BALZAC	231
GUSTAVE FLAUBERT	243
MAURICE MAETERLINCK	255
HENRI BERGSON	279
RAYMOND POINCARÉ	289

INTRODUCTION

In the Year of Terror, 1792, when the hosts of Prussia and Austria, taking advantage of the distress of their neighbours, invaded a distracted country, and initiated a European War which was to last a quarter of a century ; when France, bankrupt, without an army, and in the grip of anarchy, seemed threatened with total ruin, the greatest of German poets, who had accompanied the Teutonic legions on their triumphant march through Gaul, wrote down in his notebook, on the eve of the Battle of Valmy, the following fateful words : " On this day a new era has begun in the history of the World."

There is no Goethe amongst the German legions to-day ; there is no room for a Goethe in a Prussianized Germany. But it requires no German prophet to confidently foretell that, as on the eve of Valmy, so on the morrow of the Battle of the Marne, a new era has dawned for humanity, and that amidst the conflict of two million soldiers, amidst the thunder of thousands of giant howitzers, a new Europe is being born in suffering and sorrow. The fate of Western civilization is still trembling in the balance. In 1914 the Germans tried to force a decision in the plains of Champagne and they failed. They are still trying to force a decision in the plains of Russia in 1915, and they have not succeeded. They may to-morrow attempt to force a decision before the walls of Constantinople. Their Leviathan airships may continue to murder babies and women, their submarines may continue to sink *Lusitanias* and *Arabics*, they may continue to spread terror in every land, and to sow mines in every sea, but in the battlefields of the Marne the German coalition received a blow from which it cannot recover.

But when the final victory comes, it will not merely seal the doom of the Pan-Germanic world-power, it will not merely recast the geographical map of Europe, it will not merely mean the collapse of the two central Empires, it will not merely deliver the world from the yoke of the "unspeakable Turk," it will not merely bring transference of military and political power; it will also bring a readjustment and transvaluation of all our moral and spiritual values. "Die Weltgeschichte ist das Weltgericht," said Schiller. "Das Welt-

INTRODUCTION

gericht," the World Tribunal, has already pronounced its verdict. Even as adversity tests the moral fibre of an individual, even as disaster tests the strength and weakness of our bodily constitution, so this war has tested the strength and weakness of the body politic of every European nation. It has dispelled many an illusion. It has exploded many a theory. It has compelled us to revise many a judgment. It has revealed to us why our enemies were predestined to lose; why France, Great Britain and Russia were predestined to win.

II

POSTERITY will not cease to wonder why the German people staked a glorious present and an even more glorious future on the chances of a mad and criminal venture. They will compare the action of the German Government to that of a millionaire who would gamble away a magnificent fortune, accummulated by the labours of generations, in the Green Rooms of Monte Carlo.

At the outbreak of the war the German Empire stood at the zenith of its power. The Empire of the Hohenzollern seemed to have revived the glories of the Hohenstaufen. In the past centuries, Europe had challenged the World-Empire of Philip of Spain, of Louis XIV, and of Napoleon. But it seemed as if European nations in their very desire to avoid a world-conflict, no longer dared to challenge the German world-power, and preferred to submit to the megalomania of the Teuton rather than to plunge the peace-loving democracies into the horrors of Armageddon. Germany seemed to incarnate an implacable Destiny. Let a servile German Chancellor deliver an equivocal speech to a more servile Reichstag, and suddenly, all over Europe, the political skies were overcast. Let the Kaiser, in his restless wanderings, suddenly appear at Tangier, in Jerusalem, in Heligoland, in Norway, in the glittering armour of Lohengrin, and let him but rattle his Imperial Sword, and all the nations listened in a hush of anxious expectation.

And the commercial power of Germany had kept pace with the growth of her military power and political prestige. Through unremitting labour, through ingenious self-advertising, through iron discipline, through marvellous organization, through a mobilization of her productive forces, through a clever imitation of her rivals, through unscrupulous methods of underselling, by threat

INTRODUCTION 13

and blackmail, by craft and by graft, and last, but not least, owing to the generous free-trade policy of the British people—the Commerce and Industry of Germany were gradually ousting her rivals from every world market, and German argosies, sailing under the Black Eagle, the sinister bird of prey, carried German enterprise to the Chinese Seas and to the upper reaches of the Amazon.

Nothing succeeds like success. Nowhere had German political and commercial triumphs left a deeper impression than in Great Britain. German megalomaniacs are still indignantly reproaching the British people, supposed to be animated with base envy, for not doing justice to the magnificent efforts of their rivals. But future historians will certainly not blame Great Britain for depreciating German achievements. Rather will they blame Great Britain for unduly over-rating them, rather will they reprove her for her generous and blind appreciation.

For not only did British public opinion give Germany credit for her achievements in the province of Trade and Industry, which were real. Public opinion also extended its admiration to intellectual and spiritual achievements, which were non-existent. The trade mark " Made in Germany " had long ceased to be a badge of inferiority. In vain would dispassionate observers point out that there was no relation whatsoever between the military power of Germany and her spiritual and moral power, that a profound moral deterioration had set in, that Berlin was the most depraved capital of the Continent, that the German genius had ceased to be creative, that for the last generation German Art and German Literature had not added one single masterpiece to the inheritance of mankind. British public opinion was blind to the moral decline of the German people. Prejudice and the worship of material success were stronger than facts. Everything German was the fashion. Only German specialists could cure patients of deadly diseases, and only the bracing air and the miraculous waters of German Health Resorts had a curative virtue. The only music which found favour was the sensuous music of Wagner and the morbid music of Strauss. The only research, the only philosophy which commanded respect were German. Even estimable mediocrities like Eucken were proclaimed great original thinkers. The only seats of learning, where the British scholar could receive the consecration of his studies, were German Universities, and every theological faculty in the British Empire, from

INTRODUCTION

Edinburgh to Toronto, seemed to share Lord Haldane's belief that "Germany was the only spiritual home" for a true Briton. It was not only Kings who were made in Germany, it was not only German royalties which occupied every throne of Europe, God Almighty Himself was made in Germany. Our progressive age refused to believe in the infallibility of the Roman Catholic Church, in the religious experiences and traditions of two thousand years. But the Protestant divines believed all the more confidently in the infallibility of Professor von Harnack, Wirklicher Geheimrath and Spiritual Adviser of the Kaiser. German Higher Critics decided on their own authority, and on the authority of the Kaiser, which were the words of Christ which had to be accepted, and which were the words of Christ which ought to be rejected. And a considerable section of the German Higher Critics did not only reject the words of Christ, they did reject His very existence. The German Professor Drews, following the lead given by Strauss, fifty years ago, proclaimed that Christ was a myth, and the disciples of Nietzsche, of him who claimed to be the new Anti-Christ, declared that Zarathustra had ousted the Galilean.

III

TOGETHER with the tendency to glorify everything German, there existed a corresponding tendency to depreciate everything French. The Anti-French movement may be said to have begun with the political reaction of Burke, and the Gallophobia of de Quincey and Coleridge. It developed into the Germanomania of Kingsley and Carlyle. It found its most striking expression in that extraordinary travesty of history, Carlyle's caricature of Frederick the Great. It culminated in that odious letter to *The Times* in October, 1870, when the oracle of Craigenpuddock pronounced an inexorable *væ victis* against the vanquished of Sedan.

After 1870 a belief in the superiority of the German race, and in the inferiority of the French race, acquired almost the force of a dogma. It was assumed that the French were a decaying nation; that, with all their brilliant gifts, they were incorrigibly frivolous and incurably immoral. Critics would still ironically concede to the French a certain superiority in the arts of cooking and dancing and fashion, in the lighter graces of style. As a moral and intellectual power the French people had ceased to count. But the anti-French prejudices which gained strength in Great Britain after 1870 were not merely the outcome of German victories, and of a materialistic belief in the finality of success. It was in reality a very old British tradition. We find traces of this old British tradition even in the Olympian mind of Shakespeare—in the odious caricature of Joan of Arc, and in that characteristic passage of "Hamlet" where the frivolous young men are sent to Paris and the serious young men, including Hamlet himself, are sent to German Universities.

And that anti-French tradition was not only a deeply-rooted national prejudice against the hereditary enemy, it was even more a survival of the old Protestant and Puritan sentiment. It is true that the French people had produced the greatest of Protestant reformers, Calvin. It is true that the French Huguenots had suffered more heroically for their faith than the Protestants of any other nation, and that Cardinal Richelieu had been supporting the Protestant cause when even the Protestant Prussian Elector had deserted Gustavus Adolphus. Still the British people felt that the French nation always remained Catholic at heart, and that there exists somehow an incompatibility between the Protestant religion and the French national character. The French spirit, always aiming at universal truth, refuses to accept an exclusively national religion. French logic refuses to accord to a Book interpreted by private judgment an infallibility which was denied to the collective experiences and to the religious tradition of two thousand years. French idealism rejected the Protestant confusion of temporal and spiritual power. The French artistic sense was repelled by the iconoclasm of the Puritan reformers. French Protestantism might survive as a political party, but as a spiritual influence it has long been a vanishing quantity, and it only represented an insignificant minority in the nation.

There lay the secret to the subconscious antipathy of the British Nonconformists against France. Hence the conviction that France was doomed to be ever distracted between superstition and atheism. Hence the systematic attempt to magnify every failing of the French character, to exaggerate every political disorder.

English critics would point to the regular and progressive decline of the French population, ignoring the fact that the restriction of births was a universal law of modern civilization, and that in France the decrease was due to a higher standard of living, and even more to an increased sense of parental responsibility. Again critics would point to the increase of crime and intemperance, forgetting that crime was everywhere on the increase, and that in Germany suicide was playing havoc even amongst school-children; forgetting that drink was even more a curse in Scotland and England than in Normandy. Again, English critics would point to the political corruption and anarchy everywhere rampant, to the chronic religious dissensions, to perpetually recurring scandals such as the Panama affair, the Humbert and Dreyfus trials, the Caillaux drama—forgetting that this political and social fermentation might only be the result of a more intense political and spiritual life, of deeper conflicts between spiritual ideals; forgetting also that the struggles of democracy with their attendant risks are always preferable to the passive obedience of despotism with all its security; forgetting that the open sores of France were less dangerous than the hidden malignant disorders of Germany; forgetting, above all, that France could not be impunately the chosen ground of daring political and religious experiments without paying the price. British critics would not take the broad and philosophical and sympathetic view of the French situation. They persisted in putting the worst possible construction on every symptom, and they were congratulating themselves every day that the German and Anglo-Saxon races were not like their degenerate Gallic neighbours.

IV

WHEN the hurricane suddenly burst over France, political and military events at first seemed to confirm the most glowing anticipations of the pessimists. A few weeks before the declaration of war, Senator Humbert had disclosed the lamentable unpreparedness and the foul corruption in high places. At the outbreak of war, the insensate murder of the great leader, Jaurès, seemed as ominous as the suicide of Prévost-Paradol in 1870. The sudden collapse of military resistance, the defeat at Mons, the retreat of the French armies all along the line, seemed to justify the worst fears. In 1870 Paris, at least, had opposed a heroic resistance. In 1914 the capital was abandoned at the very approach of the enemy. In 1870 the Government had only retired to Bordeaux when the situation had become hopeless. In 1914 the French Government retired to Bordeaux within two weeks of the German invasion. Alarmists prophesied the total breakdown of the military resistance. They expected every moment to hear that the capital had capitulated: *Finis Galliae!* France was to share the fate of Poland, and like Poland she was to fall a prey to corruption and anarchy.

V

THEN the great miracle happened. Once more France manifested that recuperative power which she has revealed all through her tragic history.

At the end of the Hundred Years' War, when the country seemed at her last gasp; when the Duke of Burgundy, the greatest vassal of the French crown, the head of the younger Capetian branch, had betrayed the national cause and joined hands with the enemy; when the English invaded and occupied the whole of Northern and Central France on this side of the Loire, one of those strange events happened which make French history read like a fairy tale and a mystery play, rather than like a bald record of prosaic facts. A peasant girl of seventeen years of age arose and announced that angels had appeared to her and had entrusted to her the mission of saving the people. Joan of Arc placed herself at the head of the army, and in a few months cleared the country of the enemy.

After 450 years, once more France found

herself in the same desperate situation. Again the horrors of civil war were added to the horrors of foreign war. The insolent manifesto of the Duke of Brunswick declared that Paris would be razed to the ground. The country was bankrupt. There was no Government left and no army left. Again the nation rose in arms. Ragged bands of volunteers crushed the Prussian invader on the hills of Valmy. Once more France was saved by a miracle.

And now once more in 1914, when the country had been betrayed by incompetent and corrupt leaders, when everything seemed lost, the people arose to the national emergency, pulled themselves together. They proclaimed the sacred truce of parties. They rallied like one man in the presence of the enemy.

Yet the peril in August and September of 1914 seemed greater than it had ever been at any previous crisis of French history. Everything seemed to favour the foe. His treacherous onslaught had taken the French nation by surprise. Whilst the French armies were preparing to meet an attack on the Eastern front, the Prussian burglar had entered by the Belgian backdoor and by a frontier denuded of fortresses and troops. The enemy was reaping all the military advantages of his own crime, of the violation of Belgian neutrality, and was also reaping all the military advantages of a rigid maintenance by the Allies of the neutrality of Holland. The enemy enjoyed all the superiority of preparations on a colossal scale, of gigantic accumulations of war material. He enjoyed all the superiority of a despotic form of Government, permitting a unity and concentration of power which are impossible in a free democracy. And last, not least, the enemy possessed all the moral force of a war spirit which had been inculcated by a systematic education, and which a peaceful nation like the French could not possess. And last, not least, the enemy had all the driving power of an insensate race hatred and of a military fanaticism to which we can only find an historical parallel in the religious fanaticism of the Mohammedan hordes at the zenith of their military power.

Notwithstanding all those advantages of the barbarians, the whole military scheme of the German invader collapsed in a dramatic failure. The hosts which had swept like an irresistible tide over Northern France were suddenly thrown back in the fateful battle of the Marne, one of the decisive battles of Universal History. To-day, after twelve months, two million of stout French hearts still oppose to the invader a living wall of 400 miles. After twelve months, notwithstanding a reckless sacrifice of lives, the Germans have been battering that wall in vain. For twelve months the French have borne the brunt of the fight and the heat of the day, whilst their British and Russian Allies were getting ready for the combined counter-offensive, which was to deal the crushing blow to Prussian militarism.

VI

BUT not only did France in her hour of trial reveal a resisting power which staggered her enemies, she also revealed moral and spiritual resources which amazed her friends. She compelled us to revise all our judgments. She revealed to us how much she had learned in the stern school of adversity.

We had been told *ad nauseam* that excitability, emotionalism were the main traits of the Gallic character. And now, behold! in the darkest hour of her history she preserved a marvellous self-restraint and an impressive calmness. I was present in Paris at the beginning of August, during the first days of mobilization. I saw at the Gare de Lyon, at the Gare du Nord, at the Gare de l'Est, day and night, over one million French soldiers entrained. There was no beating of drums. There was no war fever, and I did not see one drunken man. There was no policeman to keep order, and there was no disorder in the streets. Every soldier left for the battle resolute and determined as for the performance of a solemn and sacred duty.

We had been told that the French, after an initial spurt of enthusiasm, would be found lacking in staying power ; that their effervescent temperament, which might be suitable for a vigorous offensive, for Napoleonic tactics would probably be found unsuitable for the defensive. And now, behold ! they revealed in defensive warfare the same tenacity of purpose, the same cheerful contempt of death, the same patient and stoical heroism which their Russian Allies were manifesting in the Eastern Theatre of War.

We were warned that under the influence of a succession of reverses they would succumb to the old fatal Gallic individualism, to that lack of discipline, to that incapacity for leadership, to that " spontaneous anarchy " which were bound to spell disaster. And behold ! the evacuation of Paris, the withdrawal of the Government, instead of giving a chance to the demagogues, only welded more firmly together the unity of the nation. Instead of indulging in political dissensions, every Frenchman, from the journalist to the artisan, worked in complete unanimity amongst themselves and in absolute harmony with their Allies. And the religious divisions vanished as well as the political. Twenty thousand priests were incorporated as common soldiers in the French armies. Those priests worked like heroes on the battlefield, and after the battle they ministered to the wounded like saints. There have been strikes or threats of strikes in England, in Scotland and in Wales. There have been divisions in Russia. In France the Sacred Union, the "Union Sacrée" has not been broken for one day.

VII

From the beginning of the war, in every one of her actions, in her reverses as in her successes, France has given the lie to her enemies. She has justified those who loved her and believed in her. She has disconcerted and amazed her critics. Those critics, in their surprise and in their eagerness to explain away their previous false judgments, are speaking to-day of a "new spirit," of a dramatic transformation of the French character. They tell us that the war has breathed a new soul into the people. But

INTRODUCTION 27

that explanation of the critics is as superficial as were their former blunders. What we are to-day observing in France is not something new, it is something very old and very familiar. It is the old heroism, the old vitality which are asserting themselves. The well-meaning foreign journalists, whose whole horizon was bounded by the coffee-houses of the boulevards, are amazed by this sudden revelation of order and restraint, of devotion and sacrifice. But French life in the past has ever been a miracle of orderliness and devotion to duty. Those scribblers who told us that there was no family life in France, that the French language did not even possess a word to express the idea of " home," apparently did not suspect that French family life was something very beautiful and very sacred; that even in modern Babylon there were hundreds of thousands of Middle Class homes whose whole existence was a discipline in self-sacrifice. The scribblers who sternly condemned the meanness and selfishness of the French temperament, who denounced French marriages as mercenary, who abused the French institution of the Dowry, did not know that this much-abused French institution of the Dowry was an everyday school of thrift and self-restraint and self-suppression; that from the first day of marriage, before their first child is born, the young couple are providing for the future.

But let us not be hard on those foreign critics. This is an age of prose and realism. How could it do full justice to a nation of artists and idealists? This is a calculating and scientific generation. How could it do justice to a French spirit which has ever eluded calculation, where it is the incalculable and the unexpected which always happens?

In the now distant days when misunderstandings were rife, when an important section of the English people were under the spell of Gallophobes, when France herself was distracted by civil quarrels and religious dissensions, when it sometimes seemed as if the French ship were threatened with shipwreck—a great English poet, too much neglected to-day, expressed her unshakable faith in the French people. Elizabeth Barrett Browning understood the spirit of France as few Englishmen have understood it. The following lines of *Aurora Leigh* reveal a deeper insight and contain a deeper truth than are contained in all the ponderous volumes of the detractors of French genius:—

" And so I am strong to love this noble France,
This poet of the nations, who dreams on
For ever, after some ideal good,—
Some spontaneous brotherhood.

> Some wealth that leaves none poor and finds none tired,
> Some freedom of the many that respects
> The wisdom of the few. Heroic dreams!
> Sublime, to dream so; natural to wake:
> May God save France!

VIII

Thus, O generous and gentle nation of the Gauls, did a magnanimous English singer, with the sympathy of a woman and the insight of a genius, pay thee thy just meed of praise. And to-day her inspired words are finding an echo in every British heart. There are nations whom we respect; there are other nations whom we also love. There are nations whom we both love and respect. But thee, O France! we revere with a reverence less distant and more intimate! Thee we love with a more personal and more tender love, and they love thee most who know thee best.

We admire thee for thy marvellous gifts, for thy luminous reason, for the glories of thy past, for the integrity and honesty of thy intellect, for thy romantic spirit of adventure, for the loftiness of thy courage.

And we love thee for thy grace and gentleness, for thy courtesy and chivalry; because thou hast ever been the knight-errant of every crusade, because thou hast ever been the champion of the weak and the oppressed; because thou hast ever been ready to lose thy soul in order to save thy soul and to redeem the souls of others; because thou hast ever sought the beautiful rather than the useful, wisdom rather than power, right rather than might. Already in the forests of the Druids, two thousand years ago, thy Gallic children had raised on a pinnacle the Priest and the Teacher, the Judge and the Law-maker, exalted high above the brute force of arms. All through thy heroic history, the sword of the soldier has only been wielded in defence of an idea, and military force has only been the instrument of a higher purpose.

And we love thee because of thy infinite wit and thy inexhaustible cheerfulness. Thou hast ever been radiating joy around thee. Thy heroes are smiling even in the face of death. Thy teachers, Rabelais and Montaigne, taught us that whilst pedantry is sullen and repellent, wisdom ever wears a serene and joyful countenance.

And we love thee because of thy humanity. Thou art human and compassionate to the frailties of thy children. Thou dost not claim for them a perfection which is not granted to mortal man. Thou dost not hide their shortcomings under the cloak of hypocrisy. Thy enemies have called thy children vainglorious, but even thy enemies have not dared to call them proud. Thou never didst worship a Teutonic "Superman." Rather didst thou extol the humble, the meek and the weak. Thy sociable instinct has ever taught thy children that pride is the most odious of vices, because it is the most unsociable, because it is the one vice which isolates us from the fellowship of man.

And we love thee because thou art incapable of hatred. Thy national Epics, like the *Chanson de Roland*, are poems of chivalry, of knightly deeds. The Epics of the Teuton, like the *Nibelungen Lied*, are poems of hatred and revenge. The Teutons are to-day what they were in the past. They are relentless in their rancour, merciless in their vindictiveness. And their rancour is retrospective. They cannot and will not forget. Treitschke is still brooding over imaginary wrongs committed a thousand years ago. Thou hast ever been ready to forget and to forgive. Thou dost not understand hatred. Thou dost not brandish the dagger of revenge. Thou leavest vengeance to God Almighty. Thou leavest retribution to Eternal Justice.

Enthroned in the very centre of the old Continent, in a temperate clime, under sunny skies, in thee all antagonisms are reconciled, in thee all contrasts are harmonized, all extremes are attempered. Temperance, moderation, measure, equipoise and rhythm are the hall-marks of thy genius, as they were the hall-marks of the Greeks. In thee all nations commune. In the Golden Age of the Catholic Church, twenty thousand scholars gathered within the walls of thy ancient colleges, from all parts of the world. Thy "angelic doctors" and thy "seraphic doctors" preached the universal faith. And ever since, the world has been willing to sit at the feet of thy teachers. Ever since thy Capital has been the metropolis of civilization. *Urbs orbis*.

Thou art heir to the experience of all the ages, to the wisdom of Athens and Rome. Thy spirit of adventure, thy passion for daring political experiments, thy craving for justice has misled people into thinking that thou art subversive of the past. Thy passion for truth has misled foreign critics into the belief that thou art lacking in reverence. But in no other country is the past more living. In no other country is there a more pious and grateful feeling for the achievements of her ancestors. No cult is more devoutly observed by thy people than the "Cult

INTRODUCTION 33

of the Dead." And has not one of the greatest of thy thinkers reminded us of the eternal truth that in appraising the spiritual legacy of humanity the dead must be counted more than the living.

Of all these legacies of thy wonderful past thy language is the most wonderful: simple, graceful, truthful as thy own image. It has succeeded to the universality of the language of Imperial Rome. The greatest of German philosophers and the greatest of Prussian kings only used thy language. The greatest historian of England deemed it the only fitting medium in which to write his masterpiece. The solemn covenants between nations are still written in French. In thy luxuriant youth, Brunetto Latino, the master of Dante, praised thy speech as the most "delectable" of all. In thy vigorous maturity the genius of thy children, the genius of Montaigne and Descartes, of Balzac and Victor Hugo, have added their perfections to thy speech and made it for all ages to come the vehicle of universal reason.

Far away in the Northern mists, in a Celtic land which was ever thy loyal ally, in the land of Mary Stuart, the hapless Queen who ruled over thy people, in an ancient seat of learning, it has been my privilege and pride for twenty years to worship at thy shrine, even I, the least worthy of thy worshippers. Far away from thy smiling vineyards and thy sunlit plains, I have taught others to love thee even as I love thee. I have tried to tell the young generation of the British Empire all that the world owes to thee, and I have challenged the slanderers of thy fair fame. I have tried to kindle in receptive young minds the sacred fire of thy soul. I have tried to awaken in their minds a passion for thy grace and for thy beauty.

In bygone days, it was said of thy pleasant land of Gaul that it was the most beautiful Kingdom God ever created after his own Kingdom of Heaven. Chroniclers extolled the " deeds of God through the Franks," *Gesta Dei per Francos*. For thy Frankish Kings were saints, and even thy maidens were heroes. Greatly has the world changed since those days. But thy spirit, O France, has not changed. Thy modern palaces, even as thy ancient cathedrals, still reveal thy virtues. The sanctuary of Rheims, razed by the Barbarians, was the Parthenon of Christendom. As in the days of St. Louis, of Ste. Geneviève and Joan of Arc, France is still doing the " deeds of God." Thou art still accomplishing the Divine purpose in humanity. As in the days of the Maid of Orleans, the God who ever protected thee is still choosing the humblest and the poorest amongst thy children to manifest His Divine will.

Thou hast indeed been fortunate in thy children and in thy servants. Thou hast lifted them above themselves to the level of thy ideals. There are other races which have not been thus fortunate. The ideals of nations are not always divine ideals, they are only too often heathen idols and tribal gods. It has happened in the past, it is happening even now, that all the virtues of the good and honest men amongst thy enemies have only been used to perpetrate appalling crimes in the service of those cruel tribal gods.

Even though thy children have served thee well, thou art much greater than thy children. They may wander away from thy path. Nor is thy greatness affected by their shortcomings. Thy purity has not been tarnished by their impurity, nor thy gentleness by their violence.

And that is why, O gentle and generous France, in this thy supreme hour of trial, we maintain an unwavering and unshaken trust in thy final victory. We trust in thy triumph simply because we believe in Divine Providence, simply because we cannot admit that the moral order has suddenly been subverted. Sooner far would we believe that the sun and the stars will cease to shine, and will drop from the high heavens. We are convinced in our hearts that thou shalt emerge from thy tragic ordeal as radiant as ever. The motto of thy capital—*fluctuat nec mergitur*—is engraved on every page of thy chequered annals. The bark which carried the fortunes of France, like the bark of Lutetia, has been "ever tossed on the waves, but it has never been submerged." How often in thy past history did everything seem lost! Yet thou didst keep thy stout heart and still thou didst challenge thine enemies. Thou shalt repel the Teuton as the Maid of Orleans repelled the invader. Thy men and women shall still save thee from the modern Hun as Ste. Geneviève saved thee from the Huns of Attila. Thou shalt crush the modern Prussian in the forests of Argonne as thou once didst crush the same Prussian on the hills of Valmy. And thou shalt emerge from thy trials, glorified by thy sufferings, justified by thy faith. And thy people shall continue bearing aloft the torch of Justice and Liberty, entrusted by thee to their fathers, still diffusing Joy and Beauty, Sweetness and Light, still triumphant over the the Powers of Darkness.

MONTAIGNE

MONTAIGNE

I

IN the year of our Lord 1572, the Annus Mirabilis of French history, when the massacre of the night of St. Bartholomew sent a thrill of horror throughout the civilized world, when the bells of the Church of St. Germain l'Auxerrois were sounding the death-knell of thousands of Huguenots, when his most Christian Majesty, Charles IX, and his most august mother, the Dowager Queen Catherine of Medici, were witnessing from a window of the Louvre overlooking the Seine and were directing and enjoying the holy and wholesale slaughter of their miscreant subjects, there lived in the neighbourhood of Bordeaux, at the château of Montaigne, a country nobleman of moderate fortune, of simple habits, and more noted for his learning than for those warlike qualities becoming his rank and station.

II

He claimed to be of ancient lineage and of English descent, although, if the truth be told, his grandfather was only a fish merchant. In his youth he had been a keen man of pleasure, but in his mature age he had learned to curb the passions of a sensuous temperament, and he had come to profess a profound contempt for that fair sex of which he had been such an ardent and such a fickle admirer. He was a sorry husband, which might have been the fault of his wife. He was a bad father, which certainly was not the fault of his children. He was an indifferent citizen, and there was a public rumour that, having been made a mayor of his native city, and the great plague having broken out during his tenure of office, he fled for his life, and left his fellow-citizens to grapple with the disease. He was one of those leaders of men who consider personal safety the better part of discretion, and who think that the first duty of a leader is to follow.

III

In his younger years the Lord of Montaigne had also shown an eager desire to push his way into politics. He professed to be a loyal son of the Church, and was never tired of cursing those wicked Huguenots. He was an enthusiastic admirer of the Guises, the leaders of the Catholic party, and when counsels of moderation for one moment prevailed over bigotry and fanaticism, the young man, although himself a sceptic and a pagan, went out of his way to protest against the policy of toleration inaugurated by the Chancellor l'Hôpital, in order to ingratiate himself with those in power. But he soon discovered that political honours were a burden and a danger, and that at best they were absolutely incompatible with ease and liberty, which he valued above all things. And therefore, having filled for a few years several distinguished legal offices, he decided to live in the seclusion of his own manor. And there, in the old tower, fitted up with a magnificent library, he would hold converse with one or two select friends, but especially with those quietest and most loyal of all friends, the silent occupants of his shelves. And there, whilst the whole of France was devastated by predatory warfare, overlooking from his turret the champaigns and vineyards of Gascony, he would contemplate, with philosophic composure, the political tragedy which was being enacted.

Others, indeed, might be distressed by the awful condition of their unhappy country; others, again, might be " sicklied over with the pale cast of thought "; but the temperament of the Lord of Montaigne was so happily constituted that nothing could disturb the serene

MICHEL EYQUEM, SEIGNEUR DE MONTAIGNE,
NATUS 1539, OBIT 1592.

equanimity of his disposition. It has been said that to those who are content to think, life is only a comedy; whilst to those who feel, life must needs be a tragedy. The Gascon nobleman belonged pre-eminently to the thinking kind, and not to the feeling. He had never been troubled with a morbid sensibility, and, therefore, the most harrowing horrors enacted under his very eyes would only appear in the light of a tragi-comedy of surpassing interest.

IV

And thus year after year he would pursue the equable tenor of his life, escaping, by his continuous good fortune, from all those perils which were threatening his neighbours. Once or twice, indeed, when the hurricane of civil war was surging and raging too furiously, he would think it safe for a brief moment to withdraw from the tempestuous scene, and he would prefer the stimulus and excitement of travel to the imminent dangers involved by staying at home. But as soon as the hurricane had passed over, he would repair again to his beloved castle and observatory, to his friends and to his books. And, as time went on, in the summer of his life, he would more and more give up all his days to solitude and contemplation. And, meditating on his distant travels, on the stirring events of his times, on the civil dissensions, on the discoveries and explorations of new countries, and reading those great masters of antiquity who had recently been discovered, he would write down the result of his experiences, and he would note the impressions of his readings.

And having thus garnered day by day, year after year, the rich harvest of the past, the idea naturally occurred to him that those private journals ought not to remain private, and that he ought to impart to the world the benefit of his wisdom. And encouraged thereto by the appreciation of his friends, he finally decided to publish his experiments at authorship, and those " Essays," or " attempts," as he called them, appeared in a ponderous volume in the year of grace 1580.

V

A very strange book they were, those " Essays," desultory, rambling, and, to outward appearance, rather a collection of stories and anecdotes than a treatise with a plan and purpose. They were written in every kind of style, in turn serious and frolicsome, solemn and frivolous, pious and cynical. They embraced every problem of life and death, they dealt with theology and ethics, with literature and politics. From a chapter on cannibals we pass on to a chapter on smells and public coaches; from a chapter on treason we pass on to a chapter on prayer.

And yet this strange book, by an eccentric and egotistic baronet of Gascony, thus ushered into the world in the most troubled times of the French wars of religion, has become one of the great books of world literature. The country nobleman, so careful of living in retirement and obscurity, has become one of the master-minds of his age and of all ages, " the master of those who know."

VI

The vicissitudes of literary reputations are one of the commonplaces of criticism. But we doubt whether there is another instance in the history of letters of a book having had such a singular fortune or an influence so deep, so far-reaching, so universal, so immediate, and yet so permanent. In the lifetime of the writer, when books were dear and readers were few, it attained a sudden popularity, and for more than three hundred years the " Essays " of Montaigne have been one of the forces that have moulded

CHÂTEAU OF MONTAIGNE.

European thought and literature, in substance as well as in form. The sceptical, impious, and immoral writer has become the spiritual father and guide of the most devout moralists, of the most saintly theologians. The "littérateur" and "dilettante," who knew nothing of science, has been directly or indirectly the promoter of a great scientific revival. The recluse has become the trusted adviser of men of the world. Nor is there any sign that the popularity of the "Essays" is on the wane. Indeed, the book is like the wine of the author's own Southern vineyards; it improves and becomes more "vital" as it gets older, and it becomes more valued as we get older, as we are able to interpret its lessons of wisdom from our own life experiences.

And thus the "Essays" appear to us as one of the mountain peaks of letters, or rather as a mountain range from which mighty rivers of thought have taken their source. If, indeed, you tried to bring together all the great men that have fallen under the spell of the Gascon, what an august company and what a motley crowd would be assembled: a company that would join in unexpected association Shakespeare and Molière, Bacon and Bayle, Pascal and Rousseau, Voltaire and Frederick the Great, La Bruyère and Ste. Beuve.

VII

And let us take due notice of the fact that in that illustrious company not the least illustrious names are those belonging to the history of English thought, and that the influence of Montaigne in England is not the least extraordinary feature in the miraculous fortune of Montaigne's "Essays." Here is a foreigner, a Frenchman of the French, a Gascon of the Gascons, and this alien has become to all intents and purposes an English classic, and has exerted on English literature an influence as great as that which he exerted on his own country. The work of that Frenchman, translated by the Italian Florio, has become one of the standard books of a literature which sometimes, and somewhat foolishly, boasts of its insular and splendid isolation. The greatest thinker of the Elizabethan age has been so completely steeped in Montaigne that his "Essays" would never have appeared but for the French work which served them as a model. The greatest poet of the Elizabethan age, and of all ages, has imbibed Montaigne's inmost spirit so thoroughly that he has dramatized his philosophy and plagiarized his paradoxes. Was there ever a great moralist who could claim nobler intellectual progeny than Bacon and Shakespeare, not to mention Dean Church and Emerson, Walter Pater and Fitzgerald?

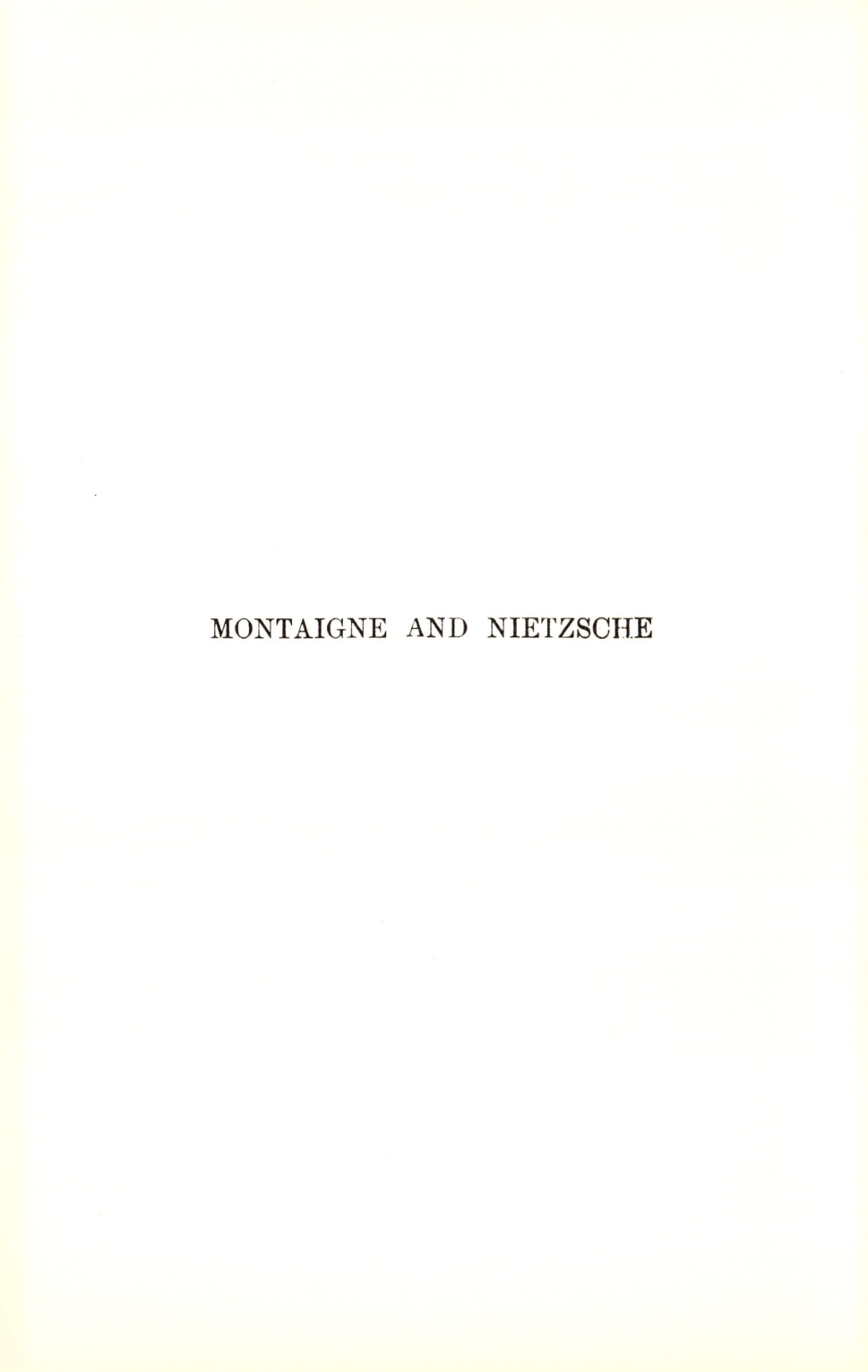

MONTAIGNE AND NIETZSCHE

MONTAIGNE AND NIETZSCHE

I

THERE is a continuity and heredity in the transmission of ideas as there is in the transmission of life. Each great thinker has a spiritual posterity, which for centuries perpetuates his doctrine and his moral personality. And there is no keener intellectual enjoyment than to trace back to their original progenitors one of those mighty and original systems which are the milestones in the history of human thought.

It is with such a spiritual transmission that I am concerned in the present paper. I would like to establish the intimate connection which exists between Montaigne and Nietzsche, between the greatest of French moralists and the greatest of Germans. A vast literature has grown up in recent years round the personality and works of Nietzsche, which would already fill a moderately sized library. It is, therefore, strange that no critic should have emphasized and explained the close filiation between him and Montaigne. It is all the more strange because Nietzsche himself has acknowledged his debt to the "Essays" with a frankness which leaves no room to doubt.

To any one who knows how careful Nietzsche was to safeguard his originality, such an acknowledgment is in itself sufficient proof of the immense power which Montaigne wielded over Nietzsche at a decisive and critical period of his intellectual development. But only a systematic comparison could show that we have to do here with something more than a mental stimulus and a quickening of ideas, that Montaigne's "Essays" have provided the foundations of Nietzsche's philosophy, and that the French Pagan may rightly be called, and in a literal sense, the "spiritual father" of the German.

II

At first sight this statement must appear paradoxical, and a first reading of the two writers reveals their differences rather than their resemblances. The one strikes us as essentially sane; the other, even in his first books, reveals that lack of mental balance which was to terminate in insanity. The one is a genial sceptic; the other is a fanatic dogmatist. To Montaigne life is a comedy; to his disciple life is a tragedy. The one philosophizes with a smile; the other, to use his own expression, philosophizes with a hammer. The one is a Conservative ; the other is a herald of revolt. The one is constitutionally moderate and temperate ; the other is nearly always extreme and violent in his judgment. The one is a practical man of the world ; the other is a poet and a dreamer and a mystic. The one is quaintly pedantic, and his page is often a mosaic of quotations ; the other is supremely original. The one is profuse in his professions of loyalty to the Roman Catholic Church ; the other calls himself Anti-Christ.

III

There can be no doubt that if the characteristics which we have just referred to belonged essentially to Montaigne, there would be little affinity between the thought of Nietzsche and that of Montaigne. And it would be impossible to account for the magnetic attraction which drew Nietzsche to the study of the " Essays," and for the enthusiasm with which they inspired him. But I am convinced that those characteristics are not the essential characteristics. I am convinced that there is another Montaigne who has nothing in common with the Montaigne of convention and tradition. I am convinced that the scepticism, the Conservatism, the irony, the moderation, the affectation of humility, frivolity, pedantry, and innocent candour, are only a mask and disguise which Montaigne has put on to conceal his identity, that they are only so many tricks and dodges to lead the temporal and spiritual powers off the track, and to reassure them as to his orthodoxy. I am convinced that beneath and beyond the Montaigne of convention and tradition there is another much bigger and much deeper Montaigne, whose identity would have staggered his contemporaries, and would have landed him in prison. And it is this unconventional and real Montaigne who is the spiritual father of Nietzsche.

It is obviously impossible, within the limits of a brief paper, to prove this far-reaching statement and to establish the existence of an esoteric and profound meaning in the "Essays." I shall only refer to a passage which is ignored by most commentators, which has been added in the posthumous edition, in which Montaigne himself admits such a double and esoteric meaning, and which seems to me to give the key to the interpretation of the "Essays":—

" I know very well that when I hear any one dwell upon the language of my essays, I had rather a great deal he would say nothing : 'tis not so much to praise the style as to underrate the sense, and so much the more offensively as they do it obliquely ; and yet I am much deceived if many other writers deliver more worth noting as to the matter, and, how well or ill soever, if any other writer has sown things much more substantial, or at all events more downright, upon his paper than myself. To bring the more in, I only muster up the heads ; should I annex the sequel I should trebly multiply the volume. And how many stories have I scattered up and down in this book, that I only touch upon, which, should any one more curiously search into, they would find matter enough to produce infinite essays. Neither those stories nor my quotations always serve simply for example, authority, or ornament ; I do not only regard them for the use I make of them ; they carry sometimes, besides what I apply them to, the seed of a more rich and a bolder matter, and sometimes, collaterally, a more delicate sound, both to myself, who will say no more about it in this place, and to others who shall be of my humour."

IV

The real and esoteric Montaigne is, like Nietzsche, a herald of revolt, one of the most revolutionary thinkers of all times. And the

Gascon philosopher who philosophizes with a smile is far more dangerous than the Teuton who philosophizes with a hammer. The corrosive acid of his irony is more destructive than the violence of the other. Like Nietzsche, Montaigne transvalues all our moral values. Nothing is absolute; everything is relative. There is no law in morals.

"The laws of conscience, which we pretend to be derived from nature, proceed from custom; every one, having an inward veneration for the opinions and manners approved and received amongst his own people, cannot, without very great reluctance, depart from them, nor apply himself to them without applause."

There is no absolute law in politics. And one form of government is as good as another.

"Such people as have been bred up to liberty, and subject to no other dominion but the authority of their own will, look upon all other forms of government as monstrous and contrary to nature. Those who are inured to monarchy do the same; and what opportunity soever fortune presents them with to change, even then, when with the greatest difficulties they have disengaged themselves from one master, that was troublesome and grievous to them, they presently run, with the same difficulties, to create another; being unable to take into hatred subjection itself."

There is no law in religion. There is no justification in patriotism. The choice of religion is not a matter of conscience or of reason, but of custom and climate. We are Christians by the same title which makes us Perigordins or Germans.

V

If to destroy all human principles and illusions is to be a sceptic, Montaigne is the greatest sceptic that ever existed. But Montaigne's scepticism is only a means to an end. On the ruin of all philosophies and religions Montaigne, like Nietzsche, has built up a dogmatism of his own. The foundation of that dogmatism in both is an unbounded faith in life and in nature. Like Nietzsche, Montaigne is an optimist. At the very outset of the "Essays" he proclaims the joy of life. He preaches the "Gaya scienza," the "fröhliche Wissenschaft." All our sufferings are due to our departing from the teachings of nature. The chapter on cannibalism, from which Shakespeare has borrowed a famous passage in *The Tempest*, and which has probably suggested the character of Caliban,

MONTAIGNE AND NIETZSCHE

must be taken in literal sense. The savage who lives in primitive simplicity comes nearer to Montaigne's ideal of perfection than the philosopher and the saint.

VI

And this brings us to the fundamental analogy between Nietzsche and Montaigne. Like the German, the Frenchman is a pure Pagan. Here again we must not be misled by the innumerable professions of faith, generally added in later editions and not included in the edition of 1580. Montaigne is uncompromisingly hostile to Christianity. His Catholicism must be understood to be the Catholicism of Auguste Comte, as defined by Huxley, namely, Catholicism minus Christianity. He glorifies suicide. He abhors the self-suppression of asceticism; he derides chastity, humility, mortification—every virtue which we are accustomed to associate with the Christian faith. He glorifies self-assertion and the pride of life. Not once does he express even the most remote sympathy for the heroes of the Christian Church, for the saints and martyrs. On the other hand, again and again he indulges in lyrical raptures for the achievements of the great men of Greece and Rome. He is an intellectual aristocrat. His ideal policy is the policy of the Spartans—" almost miraculous in its perfection." His ideal man is the Pagan hero—the Superman of antiquity—Alcibiades, Epaminondas, Alexander, Julius Cæsar.

PASCAL'S "THOUGHTS"

PASCAL'S "THOUGHTS"

I

THE launching by Messrs. J. M. Dent and Sons of a French "Everyman's Library" has been the sensational event of the publishing year.[1] It is now four years since Messrs. Nelson brought out their French Collections, over the literary fortunes of which I had the honour to preside until I assumed the onerous responsibilities of EVERYMAN. The "Collection Nelson" has become world famous, and has marked a new epoch in the French publishing trade. The Scottish invasion of France is now followed up by an English invasion. The "Collection Gallia" is continuing the work of its predecessor on a different and, I think, a more ambitious and comprehensive scale, and with an ampler scope. It is placing at the disposal of all lovers of French literature exquisite shilling editions of French classics. Immediate success has already justified this bold undertaking. The Collection was only issued a few weeks ago, and already the

[1] Written in 1914.

PASCAL'S "THOUGHTS" 61

little volumes are to be seen on every village bookstall in France and at every leading bookseller's on the Continent.

II

It was in the fitness of things that a library of French classics should begin with one of the immortal masterpieces of the language, a masterpiece which, more than any other, can claim the credit of having first fixed the standard of French style. Of Pascal's "Thoughts" there have been editions innumerable, but the present shilling edition is likely, for many years to come, to be the favourite one with the reading public. It represents the joint labours of the three leading Pascal scholars of France. Monsieur Boutroux, the master of Bergson, and leader of the new school of French philosophy (and, by the way, a close relation of President Poincaré), and Monsieur Victor Giraud, the eminent sub-editor of the *Revue des deux Mondes*, have both contributed illuminative Introductions. As for the critical text of the edition itself, it has been established by Monsieur Brunschvigg, and is the result of ten years of benedictine labour and ingenious research.

III

English students of French literature often overlook the very important fact that there are two entirely different strains running through the whole course of French literature. The most conspicuous writers are, no doubt, men of the type of Rabelais, Montaigne, Molière, Voltaire, and Anatole France, who give us, in sparkling and epigrammatic style, that incisive criticism of life which Matthew Arnold, in his famous essay on "The Literary Influence of Academies," considers as the chief function of the French mind, and who represent the purely intellectual and artistic outlook, which is so often divorced from and opposed to the moral view. It is this unbroken continuity of masters of wit and irony which has given currency to the theory that the French mind is naturally of a sceptical, cynical, and flippant turn, and that it has none of the earnestness and depth of the Teutonic mind. That theory of the superficialness of the French mind is itself based on a most superficial study of French literature. For every serious student of literature knows that, along with those masters of wit and irony, every generation of French literature has produced a succession of masters of ethical and religious little volumes are to be seen on every village bookstall in France and at every leading bookseller's on the Continent.

II

It was in the fitness of things that a library of French classics should begin with one of the immortal masterpieces of the language, a masterpiece which, more than any other, can claim the credit of having first fixed the standard of French style. Of Pascal's " Thoughts " there have been editions innumerable, but the present shilling edition is likely, for many years to come, to be the favourite one with the reading public. It represents the joint labours of the three leading Pascal scholars of France. Monsieur Boutroux, the master of Bergson, and leader of the new school of French philosophy (and, by the way, a close relation of President Poincaré), and Monsieur Victor Giraud, the eminent sub-editor of the *Revue des deux Mondes*, have both contributed illuminative Introductions. As for the critical text of the edition itself, it has been established by Monsieur Brunschvigg, and is the result of ten years of benedictine labour and ingenious research.

III

English students of French literature often overlook the very important fact that there are two entirely different strains running through the whole course of French literature. The most conspicuous writers are, no doubt, men of the type of Rabelais, Montaigne, Molière, Voltaire, and Anatole France, who give us, in sparkling and epigrammatic style, that incisive criticism of life which Matthew Arnold, in his famous essay on "The Literary Influence of Academies," considers as the chief function of the French mind, and who represent the purely intellectual and artistic outlook, which is so often divorced from and opposed to the moral view. It is this unbroken continuity of masters of wit and irony which has given currency to the theory that the French mind is naturally of a sceptical, cynical, and flippant turn, and that it has none of the earnestness and depth of the Teutonic mind. That theory of the superficialness of the French mind is itself based on a most superficial study of French literature. For every serious student of literature knows that, along with those masters of wit and irony, every generation of French literature has produced a succession of masters of ethical and religious thought—men of the stamp of Calvin, Bossuet, Rousseau, Châteaubriand, Lamennais — characters of intense earnestness and passionate fervour. Of those representative teachers and preachers, Pascal is perhaps the greatest, as he is certainly the most striking, personality in the Golden Age of French literature.

IV

About the exact chronology of that Golden Age of French literature there is still, I think, a great deal of confusion of thought. To the majority of critics even to-day that Golden Age is preeminently the age of Louis XIV. On the contrary, to a small minority the Golden Age is the age of Richelieu. I believe that it is the minority which is right. For it is the age of Richelieu which is truly the age of reconstruction and creation. It is the age which produced everything that is greatest and most original in French culture. It is the age of Richelieu which saw the rise of the French monarchy in its modern form. It saw the establishment of the French Academy and of Port-Royal. It saw the foundation by Descartes of modern French philosophy. It saw the foundation by Corneille of the French drama.

To that age Pascal may be said to belong—a giant in a generation of giants. It is true that when the " Provincial Letters " appeared Louis XIV had already been the nominal King of France for thirteen years. But at that date he was only eighteen years of age, and his personal rule had not begun. And it would be absurd if Louis XIV were allowed to appropriate the fame of a writer whose genius owes all its characteristics to the discipline of an early day, and whose writings glorify every cause which it was the policy of Louis XIV to destroy.

V

Born in 1623, from a legal stock, belonging to the middle class, like Molière, Bossuet and Racine, like most of the great writers of that so-called " aristocratic " age, a native of Auvergne, a country of extinct volcanoes and hardy mountaineers, Blaise Pascal was brought up in an atmosphere of piety and learning by a father of keen scientific tastes. The incidents of his education recall to us some of the circumstances in the upbringing of John Stuart Mill. A wonder child, with a marvellous disposition for mathematics, Pascal, at the age of sixteen, amazed even Descartes by his treatise on conical sections.

It is to be noted in this connection that Pascal's training was almost exclusively scientific, and it is certainly remarkable that this supreme master of literary style never read more than one book of secular literature, namely, the "Essays" of Montaigne, whole pages of which are incorporated and almost plagiarized in the "Thoughts."

Blaise Pascal had to pay the penalty of his morbid precocity and of the perilous overstrain of his mental faculties. At eighteen years of age his health broke down, and we are told that after this breakdown he never knew one single day without suffering. It was under the influence of his illness and of his chance acquaintance with the Jansenists that his first "conversion" took place. He became a fervid Port-Royalist, and converted his family to his faith.

The effects of this first "conversion" did not last, and for the next few years Pascal was diverted from exclusive absorption in religion by the distractions of society and by his interest in scientific pursuits. To this time belong his famous experiments confirming the theories of Torricelli.

In those early days Pascal little resembled the saint and enthusiast he was to become in later days. He was worldly and aggressive.

He quarrelled with Descartes. He quarrelled with his admirable sister Jacqueline, and wanted to prevent her from entering the convent, partly for sordid financial reasons. During those brief years also Pascal mixed freely in Parisian society. He was a friend of libertines and freethinkers. He thought of marriage, and it is presumed that to this period belongs the "Discourse on the Passions of Love." It has also been held by many biographers that the object of Pascal's love was the sister of his friend, the Duke of Roannez, but all we know about the relations between Pascal and the Duchess of Roannez is that it was on Pascal's advice that the young lady renounced the world and entered the monastery of Port-Royal.

A carriage accident near the bridge of Neuilly, in which he was saved from imminent death by a miracle, together with a moral and intellectual crisis, brought about Pascal's second "conversion." He left Parisian society and joined the solitaries of Port-Royal. He espoused their cause against the Jesuits, and in 1656 he hurled against the Reverend Fathers the first of his eighteen "Provincial Letters." A second miracle, by which his niece, Marguerite Perrier, was cured by the touch of a thorn from the crown of Jesus Christ—a relic preserved at Port-

Royal—convinced Pascal that, in defending the Port-Royalists, he was on the right side, and that Heaven was in his favour.

But a two years' ardent controversy proved too much for his highly strung constitution, already undermined. His health was ruined beyond recovery. But, together with incurable illness, ineffable happiness had come to him. Henceforward Pascal is really a new-born man. Hitherto he had been worldly; henceforth he is free from all mundane passion. He had been hard and pugnacious; he now becomes meek and charitable. He had been restless; he is now serene and smiling. He is only hard against his own self. To use the words of Professor Lanson, he "persecuted his poor body with incredible refinements of cruelty." He died in 1662, on August 19th, at thirty-nine years of age, leaving behind him the fame of one of the supreme mathematicians and physicists, as well as of one of the supreme thinkers and writers of French literature.

VI

One must accurately recall the conditions under which Pascal's "Thoughts" were composed in order not to be misled by their character.

Although conceived under the inspiration and obsession of one systematic idea, and of one settled plan, the "Thoughts" are but the disjointed notes, *disjecta membra,* scattered leaflets and sibylline leaves composed by an incurable invalid during the short luminous intervals in the course of a painful and lingering illness. Those leaflets, written with a trembling and fever-stricken hand, in almost illegible writing, were collected with pious care by the solitaries of Port-Royal, but they were of so bold and original a nature, and contained so many hostile references to the then all-powerful Jesuits, that the peace-loving Port-Royalists found it necessary to expurgate all the controversial passages. It was only in our own day that the French philosopher, Victor Cousin, discovered the original manuscript, and conclusively proved that the edition of Port-Royal of 1670 had mutilated and distorted the meaning of the writer. The first revised edition based on the manuscript was published in the forties, and tried to reproduce the original plan and design of Pascal. But it must be admitted that the attempt was an impossible one. The secret of Pascal was buried with him, and all editions, even the present one, are bound to be more or less arbitrary. The "Thoughts" of

Pascal are not only one of the most impressive ruins of world literature, they are also one of its most perplexing mysteries.

VII

It has long been assumed that the "Thoughts" of Pascal have nothing in common with the "Provincial Letters," that they are devotional rather than controversial, and that the author has transported his demonstration of the truth of the Christian religion into the sublime atmosphere of philosophical and mystical contemplation. This is not so. The "Thoughts" do not constitute a breach of continuity; they are a sequel to the "Provincial Letters." They are still strongly aggressive. Pascal is still bitterly anti-Jesuitic, and, what is more, he has become more pronouncedly anti-Roman. No doubt he is emphatically anti-Protestant, speaking with horror of the heretics who reject auricular confession. But he speaks with even greater horror of the tyranny of the Papacy. And assuredly the philosopher who again and and again, in a treatise which professes to be an apology of Christianity, goes out of his way to attack his opponents cannot be said to move in the serene region of pure devotion and mystic detachment.

VIII

We must leave over for the next chapter the discussion of Pascal's demonstration of the Christian religion, which is the prime object and purpose of the "Thoughts," and we take the liberty of referring to our discussion of the subject in our recent book on Cardinal Newman (T. and T. Clark, Edinburgh). We only wish, in conclusion, to draw the attention of the reader to what seems to us most truly original and epoch-making in Pascal's work. Critics have too much emphasized the duality between the scientist and the theologian. I do not see that the contradiction is as far-reaching as is generally supposed. To Pascal, Science and Religion are certainly different in their object; they are not essentially different in their methods. So far from Religion being opposed to Science, in Pascal's conception it becomes itself subject to scientific treatment. Religion ceases to be an abstract logical system, or a footnote to history, or an exercise in higher criticism. It becomes experimental. To adopt the terminology of William James, used by Dr. Barry: "Religion becomes a variety of human experience." The philosophy of Religion is the interpretation of the deepest intuitions and emotions and aspirations of spiritual life. And Pascal applies all the power of a marvellous intellect to the observation and analysis of those spiritual phenomena. Nor are we pressing an accidental or artificial analogy when, in connection with Pascal, we use the vocabulary of William James's famous book. For Professor James, like Professor Boutroux and Bergson, came directly or indirectly under the influence of Pascal's genius. Pascal is really the Father of Modern Pragmatism, and the "Thoughts" of Pascal may be considered as the first as well as the most profound contribution to the new philosophy of Religion.

叢書

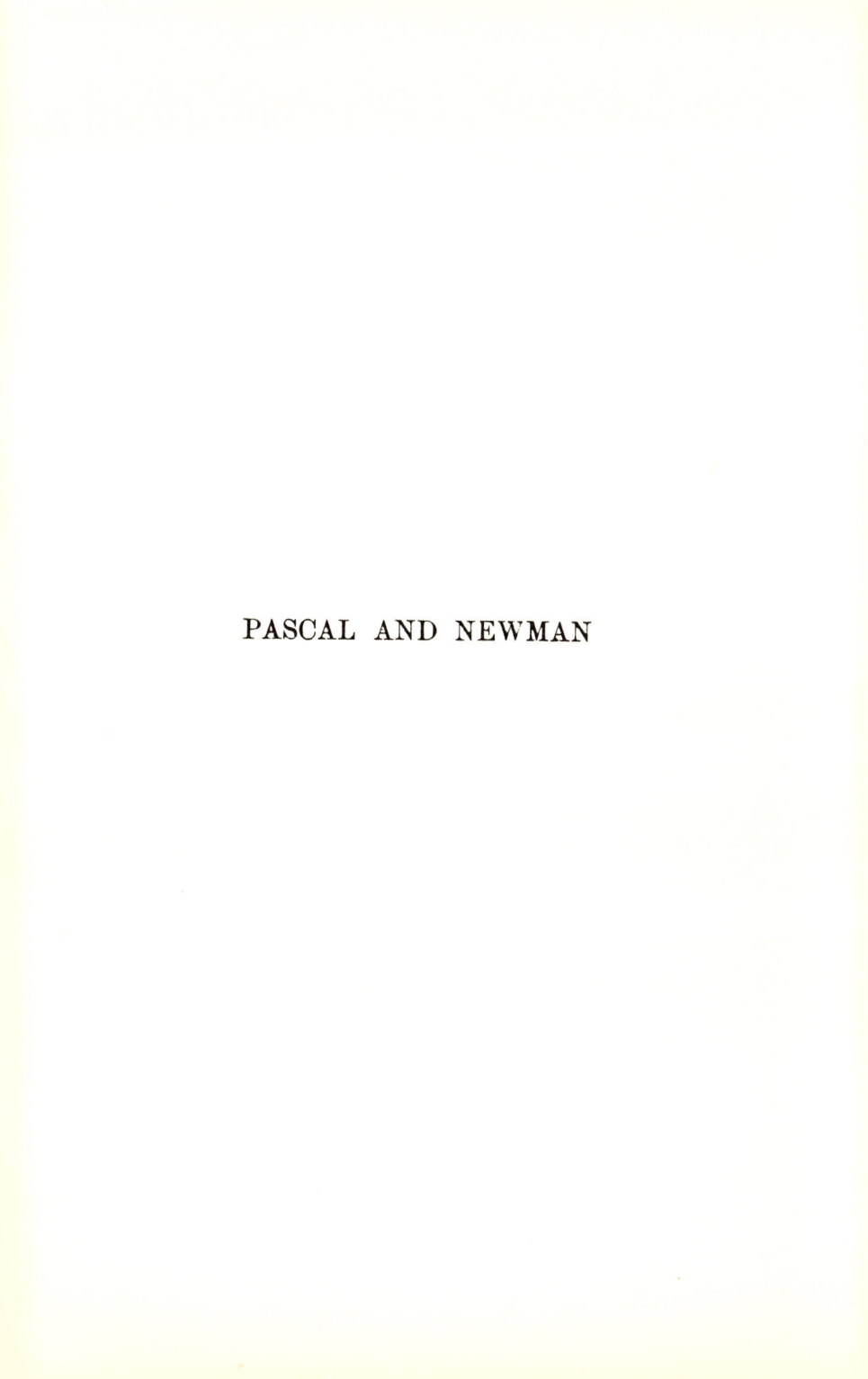

PASCAL AND NEWMAN

PASCAL AND NEWMAN

RELIGIOUS philosophy and apologetic literature in France have been nourished for the last seventy-five years on the " Thoughts " of Pascal. Since the famous " Report " of Victor Cousin, the most penetrating moralists—Vinet, Sainte-Beuve, Havet, Sully, Prudhomme, Boutroux—have applied themselves to the investigation of the fascinating and perplexing mystery.

" The Catholic Church," says M. Boutroux in his admirable monograph on Pascal, " has been for a long time satisfied with apologetic systems which are based mainly on pure reason and on authority. But to-day we witness inside the Church remarkable efforts to seek the first reasons for belief, no more in the objects of faith, but in man and in his nature. According to this method, the first condition of any demonstration of religion ought to be the awakening in the human soul of a desire to possess God, a desire which indeed constitutes one of its elemental instincts, but which is oppressed and repressed by our sensuous life. The problem would be to disentangle in nature itself the claims of the supernatural. Now it is partly under the influence of Pascal, read and meditated in the simplicity of our heart, that those aspects of Christian apologetics are being developed " (pp. 201, 202).

For the last ten years the younger generation have turned away from the problem of Pascal and have given their allegiance to Cardinal Newman; and to-day, even in France, the influence of Newman on the *élite* of Roman Catholicism is certainly stronger and deeper than the influence of Pascal. The same battles which once were fought about the *Pensées*, are being waged to-day round the *Apologia*, and the *University Sermons*, and the *Theory of Development*, and the *Grammar of Assent*. The same minds which once would follow the teachings of the one are to-day the disciples of the other. Between those two great names—the greatest, perhaps, in the religious literature of the modern world—a comparison, therefore, naturally suggests itself. Their parallel destinies correspond to the same preoccupations, the same needs of the times. And, therefore, to contrast Pascal and Newman is to probe the very depths of the spirit of the age.

And, moreover, they belong to the same spiritual family. To compare their works is one of the best means of understanding them both. We see their characteristics in their true perspective ; we distinguish those which are only secondary from those which are fundamental ; we distinguish those which are rooted in the spiritual temperament from those which are only due to the accidents of time and place.[1]

The Differences

At first sight the differences appear to be far more important than the resemblances. It would seem as if their surroundings, the age in which they lived, the circumstances of their existence, had created a gulf between them.

1. Newman is a professional Churchman, with the narrow outlook of his class ; a recluse and a monk ; a theologian writing primarily for theologians ; a convert from Anglicanism, devoting himself to the conversion of his former co-religionists.

Pascal is a layman ; a great physicist and mathematician, he has taken a leading part in the scientific movement of his time, and has immortalized his name by epoch-making discoveries. A man of the world, he writes for men

---

[1] Madame Lucie Felix Faure-Goyau was the first to point out the analogies between Newman and Pascal, as she was one of the first to introduce Newman to the French public.

of the world. What interests him in religion is not one particular sect as distinguished from another sect, but its human and universal aspect. And, therefore, he wishes to found Christianity on the bed rock of the human soul. He does not, like Newman, write for Anglicans or converts from Anglicanism; he wishes to be understood of every man; he appeals to Protestants and Catholics, to believers and unbelievers.

2. And with a wider outlook, there also seems to be a greater intensity, a deeper religious passion in Pascal than in Newman. The conversion of Pascal was rather a revolution than a gradual evolution; like St. Paul, Pascal had his illumination on the way to Damascus.[1] The "conversion" of Newman was an even, and equable, and continuous development extending over fifteen years. Newman himself confesses in his *Apologia* that his reception into Catholicism did not produce any great change in his inner life. And the change is not much more apparent in his works. For *he again makes the significant admission that in the twelve volumes of his Protestant works, where he treats of every question of*

[1] The tendency of the eighteenth-century commentators of Pascal was to emphasize the "catastrophic" nature of Pascal's conversion, and to attribute this conversion to morbid causes and to strange occurrences like the imaginary accident at the Bridge of Neuilly.

the religious life, he can hardly trace: so little difference is there between the Protestant phase and the Catholic phase!

3. Such a contrast between religious apprehension in Newman and in Pascal suggests some constitutional opposition in their temperament. Pascal is from childhood an invalid, predestined to a premature death. His life, though brief, is one long tragedy. He tells us that from his adolescence he did not spend one day without acute suffering ; and, generalizing his own individual experience, he proclaims that illness is the natural state of the true Christian. And this physical martyrdom is reflected in the tone of anguish and intense passion which is the keynote of the *Pensées*. There is something morbid, pathological, excessive, unbalanced ; something of a Christian Hamlet in the uncompromising pessimism, in the glorification of suffering, in the absence of the gentler and more human aspects of religion.

At the age when Pascal dies, Newman has not yet fulfilled one half of his career, and there still remain to him the fifty most fruitful years of his life. Monsieur Roaul Goüt notwithstanding, Newman always retained his moral health as well as his physical health ; he always impresses us, even through the most painful trials and perplexities, by his calmness, his serenity, the equipoise of his mind.

4. And these constitutional differences are expressed in the very external appearance of their works. The religious philosophy of Pascal is embodied in one little volume of scattered thoughts, written down in the intervals of suffering, fragments which the ingenuity of three centuries has been unable to piece together so as to form one consistent whole. The philosophy of Newman is expressed in forty volumes, written in the leisure of fifty years, and in the vigour of almost unbroken health; every argument in its place, in battle order; nothing left to chance, and almost every one of those forty volumes a masterpiece of composition.

The Resemblances

And yet all those differences are not as essential as they seem, and are only the result of the differences between their external circumstances. Widely as they differ in their physical constitution, they have fundamentally the same intellectual and religious temperament.

1. Both men are characterized by the same universality of mental gifts. Pascal is equally supreme in the three provinces of intellectual

activity; a great scientist, he is also a great philosophical thinker and the creator of classical French prose. Newman is a preacher and an educationist, a journalist and a controversialist, a dialectician and a theologian, a poet and a novelist. And both Pascal and Newman have placed the same extraordinary versatility at the service of the one sacred cause, on the altar of religion: Pascal has sacrificed the genius of poetry.

2. In both writers we find the same combination of contradictory qualities: on the one hand, a keen and incisive intellect, which is never the dupe of formulas and is ever ready to seize on the weak points of an opponent; the clear perception of the truths of exact science—what Pascal calls *l'esprit géométrique*—joined to the *esprit de finesse*, the perception of the finer and more delicate truths of moral science; and, on the other hand, a mystical imagination, an acute receptiveness to religious emotion, an apprehension of, and an ever-present sense of wonder and awe before the realities of the invisible world.

3. Both writers are characterized by the same fundamental originality. They are never daunted by received opinions or prejudices. Even when they are extolling habit and tradition they depart from traditional opinions.

This originality has probably been assisted in both by an ignorance truly extraordinary considering the atmosphere in which they lived. Never was there an intellect which had in it less of a bookworm than Pascal; one might almost say that the Bible and Montaigne constituted the staple of his reading. Newman as a clergyman and an Oxford Fellow and tutor had necessarily a wider culture, and he had much more of the historical mind. He was deeply read in the literature of the Fathers, but he knew little of foreign literature; he only dimly suspected the existence of German philosophy, and German theology, and German Higher Criticism, and from an early epoch he succeeded in repressing and suppressing any intellectual curiosity which might have taken him away from the contemplation of the eternal verities.

4. For indeed ignorance in both was only a result of their entire absorption in the religious ideal and their absolute detachment from mundane things. Pascal never misses an opportunity of expressing his contempt for the philosophy of Descartes. Even his own magnificent discoveries in physical science and in mathematics came to be regarded only as a passing episode.

No doubt in Newman's life we do not witness

the same painful experience of self-mutilation, and of a mighty genius committing suicide; but Newman also, as time went on, retired more and more from the busy scenes of the outside world, and led the contemplative life of the solitary monk, and he was only saved from the excesses of asceticism by his interest in education, and his duties as the Superior of the Birmingham Oratory.

5. Both writers created a new Christian " Apologia " based on a new conception of the religious phenomenon and on a new philosophy of faith. Both, warned and terrified by the demands of their own imperious intellectual instincts, used all the resources of a mighty mind to combat religious intellectualism. Religion is a disposition of the soul, a fact of experience. Religious truth is not established by the ratiocinative faculties, it is proved and realized by our lives. Faith is the supreme blossom of our moral activity. The famous phrase in the *Mystery of Jesus*, " A mesure que tu expieras tes péchés, tu les comprendras," and those other words, even more characteristic, " Cella vous fera croire et vous abétira," indicating the duty of repressing the intellect, give the keynote of the religious philosophy of Newman and Pascal.

6. Precisely because Pascal and Newman base

the truths of religion on the analysis and interpretation of our psychological experiences, their tendency is to insist on the subjective and individual aspect rather than on the ecclesiastical or political and social aspect. Whatever may be the theoretical importance which both attach to the authority of the Church and to the ministry of the priest, practically their conception of religion is mainly individualistic, one might almost say *egotistic*. As in the *Imitation of Christ*, religion is a mystical dialogue between God and the soul. The Church may provide the superstructure, conscience alone provides the foundations. In our intercourse with God we are alone, we live alone, and we die alone. In the *Apologia* Newman recurs to the words of Pascal, " Nous mourrons seuls." Neither Pascal nor Newman ever emphasizes the mediation of the priest ; the only mediator for Pascal is Christ. And for Newman there are only two realities : God and himself.

7. Both writers have adopted, in the exposition of these extreme views, the same extreme, aggressive attitude. Both are polemical writers. We must not be deceived by the conciliatory form, the courteous manner, the concessions for argument's sake. This is a mere matter of tact and policy. At heart Newman is as uncom-

promising as Pascal. He is as little content to remain on his defence or to remain sitting " on the fence," he is as ready to take the offensive and to carry warfare into the camp of the enemy; he uses as intemperate language.

8. The aggressiveness and audacity and originality of both have equally terrified their co-religionists, and have been equally misunderstood. Both have been accused of scepticism, of taking a leap in the dark, of having taken counsel from despair. In both cases the accusation is almost equally absurd. No doubt they both delight to emphasize the uncertainties of faith, to accumulate the difficulties and shadows which hide from our view the *Deus absconditus*. But in both cases the spirit and inspiration are the same; there must be something *heroic* and generous in our dealings with God. We must not attempt to drive a hard bargain. Faith must be a wager, a risk, says Pascal.[1] Faith has its *ventures*, says Newman.[2] And the more hazardous the risks, the more heroic the *venture*, the greater will be our deserts.

Notwithstanding the absurdity of the accusation of scepticism, the fact remains that

[1] See in Pascal's " Thoughts " (ed. Brunschwigg, p. 437) the characteristic pages on the *régle du pari :* Il se joue un jeu, à l'extremité de cette distance infinie, où il arrivera croix où pile . . . *Oui: mais il faut parler.*

[2] Cf. the sermon on the *Ventures of Faith.*

PASCAL AND NEWMAN

neither Pascal nor Newman can be regarded, or have been regarded, as "safe" apologists from the point of view of orthodoxy. Both have fought Protestantism as a system of religion, yet both are Protestant in spirit because they are ever ready to "protest" in the name of conscience. Is it necessary to point out the numberless passages in Newman's works on the supremacy of the religious conscience?—for instance, the famous passage in the Letter to the Duke of Norfolk on the hypothetical toast to conscience first, to the pope afterwards? Or the equally significant Letter to Bishop Ullathorne denouncing an insolent faction of Romanists? But the Protestant spirit of Pascal is no less striking, though much less known. We are to-day in a better position than were his contemporaries to interpret the hidden meaning of Pascal, as the strongest passages had been suppressed by the Port Royalists. Yet the Port Royalists were not ultramontanes. But even they could not publish such formidable "protests" as the following:—

"The pope hates and fears learned men, because they are not submitted to him by a vow."[1]

"Each time the Jesuits shall surprise the

[1] "Le pape hait et craint les savants, qui ne lui sont pas soumis par vœu."

confidence of the pope, they will cause the whole of Christendom to commit perjury."[1]

" If the Port Royalists keep silence (from cowardice) the stones will speak."[2]

" It is better to obey God than man."[3]

" If my letters are condemned in Rome, what I condemn in them shall be condemned in heaven : *Ad tuum, Domine* Jesu, tribunal appelo."[4]

" Am I alone against thirty thousand ? Not at all. You may keep on *your* side the court and the impostors. I have the truth on *my* side. She is my whole strength ; if I lose her, I am lost. Neither accusations nor persecutions will be wanting. But I have the truth, and we shall see who will win the day.[5]

10. What still further strengthens the impression of heterodoxy is that in both Pascal and Newman we find a strong leaven of Calvinism. Both have a horror of an easy religion ; both emphasize the stern aspects of Christianity ;

[1] " Toutes les fois que les Jesuites surprendont le paper, on rendra toute la chrétienté parjure."
[2] " Si ceux là se taisent, les pierres parleront."
[3] " Il est meilleur d'obéir à Dieu, qu'aux hommes."
[4] " Si mes lettres sont condamnées à Rome, ce que j'y condame est condamné dans le ciel : Ad tuum, Domine Jesu, tribunal appelo."
[5] " Je suis seul contre trente mille ? Point. Gardez, vous le cour, vous l'imposture ; moi la vérité ; c'est ma force ; si je la perds, je suis perdu. Je ne manquerai pas d'accusations et de persecutions. Mais j'ai la vérité, et nous verrons qui l'emportera."

both warn us against taking the smooth path. The Port Royalists, of whom Pascal is the advocate, are the Calvinists of the Gallican Church. And Newman himself, of Huguenot origin and educated by a Calvinist mother, has never shaken off the influences of his early training.

11. If our parallelism has not been strained to satisfy a preconceived theory, we ought to find all those striking analogies reflected both in the style of the two writers and in the influence which they have exerted—because in a great writer style is but the expression of the inmost personality, and because influence is but the interpretation of a thinker by posterity.

Now the style of Pascal and Newman present the most characteristic resemblances : both combine the intellectual qualities with the emotional, irony with pathos ; both are abstract and " spiritual " ; both have balance and rhythm, and they are musical rather than imaginative. Pascal's style is probably more impressive by its greater brevity and *lapidarity*. Both are perfectly simple and chastened— neither ever depends for effect on rhetoric ; both are not only inimitable, but they evade literary analysis because they owe nothing to artifice. *And yet both owe a great deal to art.*

Whilst producing the impression of spontaneity and inevitableness, they are yet the result of infinite labour. *Summa ars est celare artem!* We know from Newman's confession the agonies he went through in the process of writing. We know that Pascal re-wrote sixteen times some of his " Provincial Letters," and we can point to the passage at the beginning of one of the " Provinciales " where he apologizes for the length of the letter, *because he has not had time to make it shorter.*

12. And the influence of both writers proves beyond contest that several generations instinctively and independently have read the same meaning into their works. Both have turned religious thought into new and deeper channels; they have raised the moral temperature of those who have come under their spell. Consciously they have no doubt worked in the cause of Roman Catholicism in the strict sense of the word, but their influence has exceeded the limits of their Church; they have been, and continue to be, the delight alike of Catholics and Protestants, of believers and sceptics, and thus unconsciously and above all they have worked in the cause of that wider catholicism which includes all those who believe in the " Kingdom of God," and who strive to realize it in their lives and hearts.

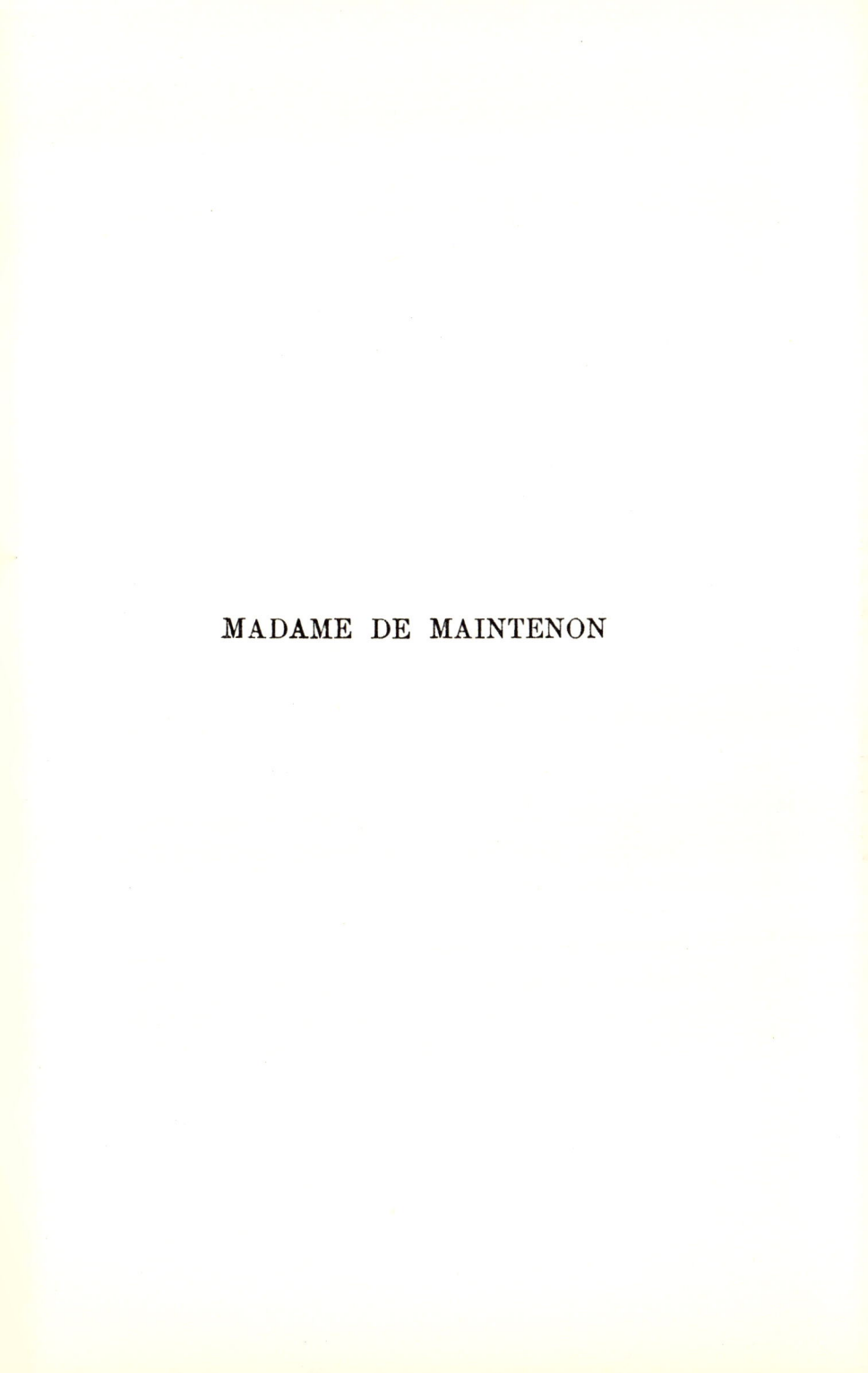

MADAME DE MAINTENON

MADAME DE MAINTENON

I

THERE are nations which are best judged by their men, nations in which it is the masculine qualities—strength of character, will power, reticence, and reserve—which predominate, where men may be considered as, physically and morally, the representative types of the race. In that sense I would call the English people, and the Teutonic peoples generally, essentially masculine nations.

On the other hand, there are nations which are best judged by their women, in which the feminine qualities of grace and charm, of wit, of exuberance and emotion, are the salient traits. In that limited sense I would call the French nation predominantly a feminine people. Certainly in no other country have women played a more important part. From the beginnings of French history, from the days of the Druid priestesses in the forests of Gaul, from the days of the women saints like Ste. Geneviève, protecting the population against the invading hosts of Attila, French women have been supreme. The ideal of woman is the inspiration of French chivalry. Again and again in mediæval history women appear in turn to save the French people, like Blanche of Castille and Joan of Arc, or to lead the country to its doom, like Isabeau de Bavière. So powerful and so dangerous was the influence of women felt to be that the French were compelled to adopt that peculiar Salic law (the origin of the Hundred Years' War), according to which no woman was allowed to ascend the throne. But no Salic law could prevent women from asserting their power and personality either as the wives, or more frequently as the mistresses, of French rulers. Diane de Poitiers and Catherine de Médici in the sixteenth century; Marie de Médici, Anne of Austria, Madame de Montespan in the seventeenth; Madame de Pompadour and Madame du Barry in the eighteenth, are only a few instances of women playing a notable part in French politics. During the Great Revolution Madame Roland was the one prominent statesman of the Girondist party. During the Reign of Terror the dagger of a girl of twenty-five ended the sinister career of Marat. Marie

Antoinette was the evil genius of Louis XVI, the ex-Empress Eugénie was the evil genius of Napoleon III.

II

Of all the brilliant women who filled the stage of French history there is perhaps no more arresting figure, none more captivating, than Françoise d'Aubigné, Marquise de Maintenon. Born in a prison, the daughter of a convict, finding herself at seventeen years of age the girl-wife of an old cripple mountebank and society jester, later a humble governess of the bastard children of Royalty, she lived to be, in an age of mistresses and courtesans, the legitimate wife of the proudest King in Christendom; and, becoming thus, a widow of forty-five, the uncrowned Queen of Louis XIV, she held captive for thirty years the most fickle of husbands by the mere magnetism of her strong personality. Into a profligate court, addicted to gallantry and gambling, she breathed a new spirit. She built model schools and institutions for the children of the impoverished nobility; she became one of the most original pioneers in the education of women. The granddaughter of Agrippa d'Aubigné, one of the heroes of Protestantism, she became a champion of

Catholic orthodoxy, a Mother of the Church, and her name has passed down to posterity, very unjustly, as the persecutor of the Huguenots, and as being mainly responsible for the revocation of the Edict of Nantes. Surely in all modern history there is no character whose biography contains in greater abundance the elements of romance, whose chequered life-story is richer in dramatic contrasts.

III

Madame de Maintenon found in her cradle a double inheritance of glory and infamy. Her grandfather, Théodore Agrippa d'Aubigné, a fanatic Calvinist, but far from being a Puritan in his conduct, a soldier of fortune, and boon companion of Henry IV of Navarre, stands out as one of the most original characters of a heroic age, and as the inspired poet of " Les Tragiques," one of the immortal masterpieces of French letters. Her father, Constant d'Aubigné, was an inveterate scoundrel, a gambler, and a debauchee. He murdered his faithless wife and her lover; he denounced his father's intrigues with the English; he betrayed one political party to the other, and was ultimately shut up in the King's prison at Bordeaux. Whilst in gaol he seduced, at forty-seven years of age, the sixteen-year-old daughter of the governor. Released from prison, he joined a band of forgers, and was sentenced to penal servitude for life. It was in the prison of Niort that the future Madame de Maintenon was born in 1635, and that she was baptized in the Catholic religion—the religion of her mother. The child was entrusted to a kind aunt, Madame de Villette, who brought her up in the Calvinist faith.

In 1642 Constant d'Aubigné was liberated and offered a post in the French Antilles, and little Françoise spent several years of her childhood under tropical skies. Her mother was a strict disciplinarian, and Madame de Maintenon used to tell in later days that she did not remember her parent kissing her on more than two occasions. Is it this absence of tenderness which explains that touch of hardness which is noticeable in all the utterances of our heroine, and is it for the same reason that Madame de Maintenon relies so little on the cultivation of the affections in the education of girls?

IV

At the age of twelve, in 1647, on the death of her father, Françoise d'Aubigné was taken back to France. On their return the family were reduced to such distress that for some time they were dependent on public charity, and the mother had to beg her food at the door of the Jesuit College of La Rochelle. Once more the kind Calvinist aunt offered to take care of Françoise, but a Catholic relative, Madame de Neuillant, interfered, and took her away from the evil influence of the heretic. The Catholic relative turned out to be a miser, and the child had to spend the best part of her time watching the geese and performing other menial services. But if Madame de Neuillant did not look after the physical welfare of her charge, she took every means to secure her conversion, resorting even to violence. She failed, and the girl was entrusted to the Ursuline nuns of the Faubourg St. Jacques. The nuns were equally convinced that the kingdom of God could only be gained by brutal treatment. There is a letter extant, the first of a voluminous correspondence spread over seventy-five years, testifying to the persecution which she had to endure. Françoise writes to her Calvinist aunt to implore her protection, and supplicating her to use her credit to save her from this convent, where life was worse than death : " Ah, my Lady and Aunt, you cannot imagine the Hell which this house, so called ' of God,' is to me, and the ill treatment and cruelty of those who have been made the guardian of my body, but not of my soul, because in that they shall not succeed. Rivette will tell you at length my anguish and suffering, as she is the only person here whom I can trust. I beseech you once more, my Lady and Aunt, to have pity on the daughter of your brother and on your humble servant."

Her aunt was powerless to intervene, and the child was left to the tender mercies of the Catholic sisters. As they saw that violence could not prevail over the strong character of Françoise, they eventually adopted gentler methods, which were ultimately successful. Françoise d'Aubigné renounced the Protestant heresy in 1649.

Thirty-five years later, the Royal husband of Madame de Maintenon employed on a larger scale those ruthless methods which had so signally failed in her youth. How shall we explain that the uncrowned Queen of France so entirely forgot the bitter experiences of her childhood, and that she did not use her all-powerful influence to cause counsels of moderation to prevail?

V

Shortly after her conversion the girl was introduced to Scarron, the greatest burlesque poet of the age. Scarron, a cleric in minor orders, and provided in his youth with many fat livings, had been struck at the age of twenty-eight with general paralysis. But even in illness his indomitable spirit did not desert him. Even as Cervantes wrote " Don Quixote " in prison, the lame poet from his couch poured out a continuous stream of burlesque masterpieces, and through the brilliance of his conversation and his irrepressible wit he gathered round him the most select society of Paris.

We know little about the early relations of Scarron to Françoise d'Aubigné. Madame de Maintenon, in later days, was, naturally, very reticent on this period of her life. All we know is that the cripple fell in love, that with characteristic generosity he offered to provide a dowry to enable her to enter a convent, that she refused, that he offered to marry her, that she accepted, and that she married, before she was seventeen, a helpless invalid who was three times her age. In such a marriage there could be no question of love. It was a "marriage de raison." Madame Scarron was at seventeen what she remained all through life, sensible, practical, seeking happiness in renunciation. And she partly found happiness. At least this monstrous union of an old cripple with a beautiful girl of seventeen had its compensations. If the young wife was the faithful nurse of the husband, the husband was an indefatigable teacher of the wife. He taught her Italian, Spanish, and Latin. He taught her the art of conversation, in which she was to be supreme. And as he was a fellow of infinite wit, he continued to attract the leaders of Parisian society who were to befriend Madame Scarron in later life. Altogether it is this strange marriage which laid the foundation of her prodigious fortune.

The poet Scarron died in 1660, and at twenty-five years of age his widow was left almost penniless. But she had made powerful friends, and through their influence she received a pension of 2,000 livres, which was an ample provision for her modest needs.

The greatest memoir-writer, St. Simon, and the most entertaining letter-writer of the age, the Duchess of Orleans, who both pursued Madame de Maintenon with an undying hatred, inform us that during her widowhood Madame Scarron accepted the favours of several noblemen, notably of the Marquis de Villarceaux. The accusations of St. Simon have been repeated and accepted by most historians, but they have been proved to-day to be entirely devoid of foundation. They are not supported by any contemporary witness and they are refuted by such unexceptionable witnesses as Madame de Sévigné and the Chevalier de Méré. "We are having supper every night with Madame Scarron," says Madame de Sévigné. "She has a delightful wit, and her intellect is marvellously reliable. It is a delight to hear her argue, and she is fascinating company."

But, apart from such irrefutable testimony, the slanders of St. Simon are intrinsically improbable. It is inconceivable that a young woman of doubtful reputation should have been chosen to educate the children of Louis XIV, nor are St. Simon's statements reconcilable with what we know of Madame Scarron's character. She did not pretend to be a saint, but all through life she had a rigid sense of honour. She sought esteem even more than admiration. In later years she dilated to her pupils on this craving for worldly approval—the mainspring of her moral life : " I wish I had done for God what I have done for the world, in order to preserve my reputation. Yet this love of worldly esteem, even though it is mixed up with pride and vanity, and although it must have the corrective of religious feeling, is nevertheless very useful to girls. It helps to preserve them from the disorders of passion, and for that reason I would never advise any educator to suppress it in the heart of youth."

VI

In 1669 the decisive event of Madame Scarron's life took place. She was selected as the governess of the illegitimate children of Louis XIV and Madame de Montespan. The reigning favourite had made Madame Scarron's acquaintance at the house of a common friend, Marshal d'Albret, and had learned to appreciate her sterling virtues and her peculiar qualifications for the delicate functions with which she was now to be entrusted. Madame Scarron was eminently tactful and discreet, and tact and discretion were all the more necessary as the children of Madame de Montespan had to be brought up in the utmost secrecy. Louis XIV would probably not have minded challenging public opinion, but he did not dare to defy the Church and publicly to acknowledge the offspring of his amours. A small mansion was taken for Madame Scarron in a secluded suburb of Paris, and there for years she led a double life, and even her intimate friends had no suspicion of the responsible post to which she had been called.

And not only was Madame Scarron tactful and discreet; she had the maternal instinct. She who was destined never to have any children of her own passionately loved children, if the word passion may fittingly be applied to a personality so entirely self-possessed. She was a born governess and an ideal nurse. She had spent eight years of her youth in tending a middle-aged cripple. She was to spend the next ten years in training the bastard little princes. She was to spend thirty years more in attending the old King. And in the days of her favour any leisure which was left her after her onerous duties at Court she devoted, at St. Cyr, to the education of the daughters of indigent noblemen. When the courtiers of Versailles thought her mainly bent on advancing her own fortune and those of her relatives and friends, she was busy in attending to the most minute details of management of the great school she had founded.

VII

At the beginning Madame Scarron felt duly grateful for the patronage of the all-powerful favourite, but soon difficulties began to arise. Madame de Montespan was an unwise mother, in turn unreasonably hard and fondly indulgent, and her domineering and wilful temper made the task of the governess both more irksome and more difficult. The difficulties increased when Madame de Montespan began to notice that the King was paying marked attention to the fascinating widow. Distrust and jealousy were added to caprice and incompatibility of character. Violent scenes took place almost every day, echoes of which are to be found even in Madame de Sévigné. The position of Madame Scarron was becoming untenable.

When and how did the estrangement begin? When did Madame de Maintenon begin to attract the attention of the King? And was it the King or the widow who made the first advances? If we are to believe St. Simon, at first Madame Scarron rather repelled than attracted Louis XIV by her austerity and her lack of humour, and the King repeatedly told his mistress to dismiss the governess. He obstinately refused to reward her for her services, and it was only after the most persistent demands on the part of Madame de Montespan that he made her a grant of 250,000 livres and gave her the means of buying the estate which was to transform Madame Scarron into the Marchioness de Maintenon.

It is a story difficult to believe, and it is almost as difficult not to believe it. If it is not true, St. Simon becomes a deliberate liar, and we must discard the greatest Memoirs of all times as a tissue of falsehood. On the other hand, if the story is true, it seems as if we ought entirely to change our estimate of Madame Scarron's character. For she would have repaid Madame de Montespan's generosity with the basest ingratitude. She would have deliberately planned from the first to oust a kind friend and protectress, to whom she owed everything, from the affections of the King.

But we need be in no hurry either to accuse Madame Scarron of base ingratitude or to accuse St. Simon of conscious falsity. Madame de Montespan may have been genuinely friendly at first, but she may have undone all her acts of kindness by her uncontrollable outbursts. Madame Scarron may have been sincerely grateful at first, but she may have found it impossible to submit to the caprices of an imperious tyrant. And she may have only discovered imperceptibly her growing influence with the King, and, having once discovered her power, she would have been more or less than human if she had allowed her former feelings for Madame de Montespan to stand in the way. Her position at Court was already very strong when, in 1673, Louis XIV publicly acknowledged his children, and when their nurse became officially the " gouvernante " of the Royal princes. Her position was further strengthened when she bought the estate and received the title of Maintenon. Nor need we attribute any special magnanimity to Madame de Montespan when she forced the claims of Madame Scarron on her lover. She may have scented the danger and dreaded a possible rival, and she may have wanted to get Madame Scarron out of the way. She may have hoped that, once the governess were in a position to leave, she might be tempted to resign an uncongenial post. One thing is certain, Madame de Maintenon did not fulfil the expectations of the favourite. She had often threatened to leave, but thought no more of carrying out her threat. Henceforth, with an official position, with a title and a competence, Madame de Maintenon remained. She submitted to the ill-will of the favourite, being secure of the good-will of the King. She knew that her day was coming.

VIII

For as she was gaining ground, Madame de Montespan was losing. She indulged more and more her ungovernable temper. She was making scenes not only with Madame Scarron, but with her Royal lover. She became more and more extravagant. In a few hours she would squander a fortune at the gaming table. She presumed too much on her waning charms, nor did she realize that her pride had made her countless enemies at Court, who were interested in bringing about an estrangement. About 1679 the estrangement must have been nearly complete, for about this time we find two other rivals in favour, Madame de Fontanges and the Princesse de Soubise, and we find Madame de Montespan making desperate efforts and resorting to criminal means and to "Black Magic" to regain the affections of her fickle lover.

Those were the golden days of palmists and clairvoyants. Those also were the days of professional poisoners. Madame de Montespan believed in love philtres and love powders. She believed in witchcraft and in the Black Mass, and, in order to get a rival out of the way, she did not hesitate to call in the services of an infamous criminal, la Voisin. In 1680 what is probably the greatest poisoning trial of all times staggered the conscience of France. A succession of heinous and unmentionable crimes were brought to light, and it was revealed that the favourite of the King had given her confidence to the woman la Voisin, and had made free with the name of the King. The affair was hushed up, but any lingering affection which Louis XIV might still have felt for his mistress vanished. The spell of Madame de Montespan was broken.

IX

In 1681 the doom of Madame de Montespan was sealed, and in 1683 the Queen died. Henceforth the place was free for the new favourite. Six months after the Queen's death Madame de Maintenon became the morganatic wife of Louis XIV. It was Madame de Maintenon's destiny, in her days of glory as well as in her days of humility, always to be placed in a false position. She was in a false position as the girl-wife of an impotent cripple. She was in an equivocal position as the governess of the bastard children of Royalty. She still remained in a false position as the uncrowned Queen of France. She was the wife of the King, but she was only the morganatic wife. Officially she had to be content with a back seat. Officially she was only a Lady-in-Waiting to the Dauphiness. But in reality she occupied the first place in the kingdom. For thirty years she was the trusted adviser of Louis XIV. She transformed the fickle lover and frivolous pleasure-seeker into a pious and devout ruler. Not only was she the inseparable companion, she became the religious conscience of Louis. It is to her that he owed his "conversion."

X

The conversion was hastened by a severe illness, and both the conversion and the illness had ominous consequences. In 1686 Louis XIV submitted to a severe operation. For months the Court surgeons had hesitated to incur the risk, and had ransacked all the hospitals of France and performed similar operations on hundreds of patients in order to try their hand. For months after the operation the life of Louis hung in the balance. It is the characteristic of despotism that the most trivial incidents may produce the most incalculable results, and the illness of the King did produce incalculable results. Michelet has rightly divided this long reign of seventy-two years into two periods: before the operation and after the operation. In the days of his strength Louis had been called upon by Bossuet and Bourdaloue to surrender his mistress, to cease causing scandal to his subjects, but he had refused to listen. In the dark days of suffering, in the presence of death, he saw the evil of his ways, and he determined to do penance for his sins. And he did vicarious penance at the expense of hundreds of thousands of his subjects. Because he had sinned, the Huguenots were to suffer.

The whole of the French people supported the religious policy of the King. The Huguenots were odious both as heretics and as rebels. Not only the gentle Fénélon but the sensible Madame de Sévigné were in favour of the Revocation. Even the persecuted Jansenists, even Nicole, were enthusiastic in praise of the new Constantine, in praise of a policy which inflicted untold sufferings on hundreds of thousands of innocent victims, and which sent those victims as exiles to the extreme ends of the earth.

XI

The influence of Madame de Maintenon has been very much overrated. She was not ambitious, and she preferred remaining behind the scenes. She avoided the responsibilities of power as anxiously as others sought them. She meddled neither with the Foreign Policy nor the Domestic Policy. Her only interests were in educational and religious matters. She did not care who was to be in command of an army or in charge of a ministry, as long as she was consulted on the selection of bishops and cardinals. She took an active part in the theological quarrels which loomed so largely in the second half of the reign. She took the side of the Jesuits against the Jansenists, she took the side of Bossuet, whom she distrusted, against Fénélon, whom she loved.

Her last years were darkened by public disasters. The Revocation of the Edict of Nantes and the English Revolution had ushered in twenty-five years of almost uninterrupted wars, at the end of which France found herself reduced to a state of bankruptcy. Private tragedies were added to public misfortunes. Death removed, one after another, the Princes of the Royal family, first, the only brother of Louis, the Duke of Orleans, then his only son, lastly, his two grandchildren, and his granddaughter, until the dynastic succession was only insured by one infant great-grandson, the future Louis XV, of infamous memory. Louis XIV bore these private and public calamities with heroic fortitude. The pride of former days had mellowed into a quiet dignity which called forth the loyal admiration of his subjects and the respect of his enemies.

Louis XIV died in 1715; Madame de Maintenon only survived him by four years.

He had reigned for seventy-two years; for thirty years she had shared his throne.

With characteristic discretion, Madame de Maintenon left the palace twenty-four hours before the King's death, and withdrew to her beloved St. Cyr. She found herself, at eighty years of age, ruling an institution of girls with the same tranquil firmness with which she had ruled the Court of Versailles. Her enemies had accused her again and again of having amassed prodigious wealth. It was discovered after her death that the total personalty left by the uncrowned Queen of France amounted to a few hundred pounds.

LISELOTTE

LISELOTTE:

A German Princess at the Court of Louis XIV

I

ABOUT the end of the seventeenth century there lived at the Courts of Versailles and St. Cloud a German Princess, the second wife of the only brother of Louis XIV, who had made herself the butt of universal ridicule. Strikingly ugly, tactless in manner, coarse in speech, cynical and sarcastic, she was despised and derided by the courtiers, she was ill-used by her husband, she was out of favour with Louis, she was hated by the King's morganatic wife, Mme. de Maintenon, the uncrowned Queen of France. In the busy throng which filled the galleries of the huge palace, she lived, in the recess of her private apartments, an existence of almost complete solitude, and eventually she was reduced to the company of her dogs, which she preferred to the society of a Court which she abhorred. Her chief occupation in life for thirty years was to write interminable letters to her relatives and friends in Germany, and in those letters she would not, like her contemporary Mme. de Sévigné, pour out the fullness of an affectionate heart; she only sought an outlet for the malignant German hatred that oppressed her. Little did the courtiers suspect that the ungainly, massive, unpopular Princess was to be the ancestress of half the Imperial and Royal houses of Europe, and that she would appear to posterity as one of the most remarkable women of her age. Still less did they suspect that their own reputations would be at the mercy of a woman whom they reviled, and that she was drawing the features of their moral characters in indelible lines for all times to come.

II

The voluminous correspondence of Elizabeth Charlotte, Duchess of Orleans, better known to French historians as " Madame," and known to German historians under the endearing nickname of " Liselotte," form with the " Mémoires " of Saint Simon the most important historical document for the last thirty years of the reign of Louis XIV. From a purely literary point of view, the Memoirs of Saint Simon are, no doubt, vastly superior, and it would be absurd to compare the finished, incisive pen-portraits of the greatest memoir-writer of all ages with the slovenly, formless outpourings of Liselotte. But from a purely historical point of view, the Correspondence of " Madame " has even greater value than the " Mémoires," for these only received their final form fifty years after the events they narrated, and the historian writes mainly from hearsay, and indirect report. On the contrary, the letters of Liselotte were written day after day under the direct impression of the events she described. She possessed, moreover, unique opportunities of knowing the chief personages of the times, and she was a far better observer, as well as a more intelligent one, than the narrow-minded Duke. And, finally, being a German of the Germans, and thus observing the Court of Versailles, as it were, from the outside, her judgment was more detached, as well as more penetrating.

Whilst there exist considerable differences and disagreements between the " Mémoires " and the " Correspondence," at the same time there also exists a striking parallelism between them. Both writings owe their origin to the same circumstances, namely, to the fact that Saint Simon and Liselotte were both seeking, in their productions, an occupation for their enforced leisure and an outlet for their passions, their grievances and disappointments. Both had to hide their writings from their contemporaries. Both writers are bent on depicting the darker side of Court life. Both look on the chief characters and events of their generation from the same angle.

And both the "Mémoires" and the "Correspondence" have been buried for several generations in the secret archives of France and Germany. It is only in our own day that M. de Boislisle has been able to give us a complete edition of Saint Simon. As for the three or four thousand letters which make up the "Correspondence" of "Madame," they are still partly unpublished. No doubt, publication after publication have appeared at different times. The Literary Society of Stuttgart has published no less than seven volumes. The great historian Ranke has edited a whole volume as an appendix to his French History. But a considerable fraction of the letters are still hidden in various German private and public libraries, and we are still waiting for the enterprising editor who will give us the complete and standard edition. The extraordinary success which has recently attended the publication by the " Langewiesche Buchhandlung " of a most interesting selection from the " Correspondence "—no less than twenty-five thousand copies have been sold—testifies to the growing public interest in one of the most remarkable characters and one of the most valuable historical documents of modern times.

III

The young German girl, who arrived in 1672 at the Court of Versailles, at nineteen years of age, as the bride of " Monsieur " Duke of Orleans, and only brother of Louis XIV, belonged to one of the poorest but one of the most illustrious dynasties of the Empire. Her father, Charles Louis, Elector Palatine, had recovered his principality on the Peace of Westphalia in 1648. Her grandfather, the head of the Protestant Union during the Thirty Years' War, and the ephemeral and ill-fated King of Bohemia, was a descendant of William of Orange, and the husband of Elizabeth Stuart, daughter of King James I of England. It is not generally known that, through this marriage, Mary Stuart has become the ancestress in direct line of practically every European dynasty,—of the German and Austrian Emperors, of the Kings of England, of France, Spain, Belgium, and Bulgaria. An uncle of Liselotte, Prince Rupert, had distinguished himself in the English service. Another uncle married the notorious Anna of Gonzague, the "Princess Palatine." Her Aunt Sophia was the mother of King George I of England.

The rich valleys and vine-clad hills of the Rhine Palatinate had been left at the end of the Thirty Years' War in a frightful state of devastation. The population had reverted to barbarism and cannibalism. The political anarchy and the moral confusion were as great as the material ruin. All laws and traditions were in abeyance, and were overruled by the tyranny and personal caprice of petty princes. We shall find Liselotte passing merciless judgment on the manners and morals of the Court of Versailles, but the morals of the paternal Court of Heidelberg were not much better. Her father, being unable to agree with the wife whom he married in 1650, dissolved the marriage on his own authority in 1658, and, having the supreme control of the Church as well as of the State, he forced his subjects to recognize his bigamous union with Louise von Degenfeldt. The Church Courts accepted the strange situation, even as Luther had sanctioned the bigamous marriage of Philip of Hesse. Poor Louise proved a most compliant and long-suffering wife, and she bore her lord fourteen children. For many years the two wives lived together in Heidelberg, and the little Court was the theatre of endless domestic quarrels.

It was fortunate for Liselotte that at the early age of seven she was removed from those strange family surroundings and was entrusted to the affectionate care of her Aunt Sophia of Hanover. One of her first letters, written when she was seven years of age, informs us that in 1659 she visited her grandmother, Elizabeth Stuart, who lived as an exile in Holland. The ex-Queen of Bohemia presented her granddaughter with a little dog, with a dancing-master, and a language-master. She also made her a promise of a singing-master.

The four years spent at the Court of Hanover were the four happiest years of Liselotte's life. Until the end of her days she will revert to that blissful period, and she will retain a passionate affection, not only for her Aunt Sophia, but for all those who took part in her early education.

In 1663, her father, Charles Louis, finally succeeded in getting rid of his first wife, and in securing her removal to Cassel. Liselotte could now safely return to the paternal home, where she grew up with a numerous progeny of illegitimate step-brothers and step-sisters. It is characteristic of her good nature that she always maintained the most cordial relations with all her father's second family. Indeed, she grew to love her step-brothers better than her lawful brother, the future Elector Palatine.

IV

Life at the Court of Heidelberg was a queer mixture of dullness and pomposity, of pride and poverty, of freedom and tyranny. Charles Louis was a martinet, and a pedant, thrifty and stingy, indulgent to himself, implacably severe to his children and to his subjects. Being a good manager, he soon succeeded in restoring the prosperity of his country; but his political position remained difficult and precarious between the German Emperor, who was his nominal sovereign, and the King of France, who possessed the controlling power in the German Federation. Every means was deemed legitimate by Louis XIV to increase his influence. He did with the German Courts what he had done so successfully at the Court of Charles II. He used in turn the intrigues of his diplomacy, the power of money, and the fascination of beauty. Pensions were lavished on impoverished princes. French mistresses and French dancing-masters were freely sent and exploited for political purposes.

It was the need of strengthening his political position as well as the desire to get his daughter out of the way that determined the Elector to seek a matrimonial alliance with the French Court, on the sudden death, in 1671, of Henrietta of England, wife of the Duke of Orleans.

Little did the Elector Palatine foresee that the marriage of his daughter would prove to his country, not a source of strength, but a cause of disaster, that Louis XIV would use the claims of Liselotte as a pretext for invading her father's country, that the Palatinate would be pillaged once more by hordes of soldiers, that the Palace of Heidelberg would be burned to the ground, and that all those horrors would be perpetrated on the pretence of asserting the rights of the Duchess of Orleans. He might have been put on his guard by the very eagerness with which the German marriage was welcomed by Louis XIV. The proud King would not have been so keen to accept the proposal if he had not already harboured political designs of his own. Not only was he then bent on extending his influence in Germany, not only was he coveting, like his predecessor Francis I, the crown and sceptre of the Holy German Empire, but he was determined to use Liselotte as a pawn in the game of politics, and eventually to establish a claim to the succession of the Palatinate.

But those consequences of the German marriage were still distant and remote, hidden in the womb of Destiny. In the meantime, to all outward appearances, Elizabeth Charlotte was making a brilliant match. The marriage contract was arranged on terms the most favourable to the Elector Palatine. What was a most important matter for an avaricious Prince like the Elector, encumbered with a numerous progeny, a dowry was not insisted on, and even the nominal sum which had been promised was only paid after many years' delay. And not only did Liselotte enter France without a dowry, she did not even receive a trousseau. It was a matter of deep humiliation to the proud young Princess that her father sent her to Saint Germain with a most inadequately supplied wardrobe. The sole condition which Louis XIV insisted on was a change of religion, and that was more easily obtained from the Palatine Prince than an adequate provision of money. A Duchess of Orleans must needs be a Catholic.

Charles Louis, although one of the leaders of the Protestant party, thought, with Henry IV, that Paris and the Palais Royal and the Palace of Saint Cloud were well worth a Mass. To save appearances, and to make matters easier for her father, poor Liselotte had to act her part in an ignoble comedy. Nothing was said in the marriage contract about a change of religion, and she was supposed to be converted of her own free will. It was arranged that on her arrival in France a letter was to be dictated to her, in which she was to announce to the Elector her voluntary conversion. Her father was to send in reply a letter expressing his righteous indignation at his daughter's apostasy from the true Protestant faith. . . .

After all, we need not wonder at Liselotte's strange conversion. It was only an application of the old Lutheran principle adopted from the very beginning of the Reformation:—Cujus regio, illius religio." Religious allegiance followed political allegiance, and spiritual interests were subordinated to reasons of State.

V

The husband to whom the simple German girl was married had a most detestable reputation.

Public rumour accused him of having poisoned his first wife, Henrietta of England, whose sudden death has been immortalized in the " Oraison funêbre " of Bossuet, "*Madame se meurt! Madame est morte!*" And although that accusation has been disproved, the evil repute of " Monsieur " was otherwise amply deserved. All spirit and manliness had been crushed out of him by Cardinal Mazarin. The younger brothers of the French Kings had often given trouble in previous generations. In recent times Gaston of Orleans had been one of the leaders of the Civil War. Mazarin, therefore, had been above all careful to make " Monsieur " a harmless fool and a compliant tool of his elder brother. He had only succeeded too well.

"Philippe, Duke of Orleans," says Saint Simon, " was a little round man, who seemed mounted on stilts, so high were his heels. Always decked out like a woman, covered with rings, bracelets, with jewels everywhere, and a long wig brought forward and powdered, with ribbons wherever they could be placed, highly perfumed and in all things scrupulously clean, he was accused of putting on a very little rouge. The nose was very long, his eyes and mouth fine, the face full, but long."

" Madame " herself points out the striking

contrast between the Duke of Orleans and Louis XIV, entirely to the disadvantage of her husband. " One would never have taken the King and ' Monsieur ' for two brothers. The King was tall, whilst My Lord was short. He had purely effeminate inclinations, was fond of dress, was careful of his complexion, loved every kind of female occupation and ceremony. The King was quite the opposite. He did not care for dress. He had only manly tastes. He was fond of shooting, and liked to talk about war. ' Monsieur ' behaved well on the battlefield, but he did not care to talk about military matters. ' Monsieur ' loved to have ladies as playmates, and delighted in their company. The King preferred to see ladies more privately, and not in all honour like ' Monsieur.' "

VI

With characteristic outspokenness, "Madame" admits that "Monsieur" was sorely disappointed on first meeting her. He expected a plain bride, but the reality exceeded his anticipations. "When I reached St. Germain, I felt as if I had dropped from the sky. I put on as pleasant a face as I possibly could. I saw full well that I did not please My Lord and Master, but there was no witchery in that, considering how ugly I am. So I took the resolution to live with him so amicably that he would get accustomed to my ugliness, and put up with me, which, in fact, is what actually happened."

However, the first years of the marriage were not unhappy. " Monsieur," if not affectionate, was deferential. " Madame " was sensible, and indulged her husband's weaknesses. Both agreed to differ. " Madame " received many a pleasant visit from her friends and relatives in Germany. Both her brother, Charles Louis, and her beloved aunt, Sophia of Hanover, came to Versailles, witnessed Liselotte's growing favour, and basked in her popularity. The birth of three children proved a firm bond between a couple who otherwise had nothing in common.

VII

After about six years of married life, relations became gradually strained. But even then " Madame " found ample compensation in the friendship of the King. Louis found pleasure in the sallies of his sister-in-law. He appreciated her outspokenness, her sound judgment and common sense. He relished her quaint language and her strong German accent. He delighted in taking her out hunting, in making her his confidential adviser. On the other hand, "Madame" felt unbounded admiration for his Majesty. If we are to believe the gossip of the Court, as we find it retailed in the Memoirs of the times, in the "Correspondence" of Mme. de Sévigné, and if we read between the lines of "Madame's" Letters, she very soon got to feel something more than friendship and admiration for Louis. It was the King who had fallen in love with the first Duchess of Orleans : now it was the second Duchess who fell in love with the King. There is at least this advantage in Mme. de Sévigné's version, endorsed as it is by the most recent biographer of Liselotte, Mme. Arvède Barine, that, if we accept her view, it becomes much easier to understand the unbounded hatred which Liselotte came to feel for Mme. de Maintenon. That hatred was not due to any incompatibility of temperament, or to wounded vanity, rather did it originate in female jealousy. The "Widow Scarron," the "Sultana," the "witch," had ousted Liselotte from the affections of King Louis.

VIII

After the birth of her daughter, in September 1676, a complete change took place in the relations of "Madame" both to her husband and to her brother-in-law. "Monsieur" fell more and more under the influence of his minions, and subjected his wife to petty humiliations. The King ceased to pay her attentions. He ceased to take out his sister-in-law for drives to Marly and hunting parties in the forest of Fontainebleau.

Liselotte attributes the change to the intrigues of the minions and of the odious "Sultana." The truth is that the cause of the estrangement lay much deeper than mere personal machinations.

In the first place, there were the racial differences between the French character and the character of Liselotte, which was thoroughly German. Unlike most Germans, who so easily merge their national peculiarities, she refused to be assimilated, to adapt herself to the atmosphere of the Court. She retained her idiosyncrasies. With truly German tactlessness and indiscretion, she criticized every French custom and institution. Imbued with an overweening pride of birth, she insisted on her prerogatives. She was intractable in matters of etiquette. She proclaimed the superiority of the ancient German nobility over the upstart French " Noblesse." She even claimed superiority for German sausages and German sauerkraut over the refinements of the French cuisine. She was merciless in her judgments of the leading personages at Court, and, as her letters were periodically opened by the post and copied in the " Black Cabinet," she made herself, in a very short time, countless enemies.

Nor must we forget the fatal effect produced by her outspokenness in matters of religion. " Madame " was a most liberal Christian, and almost a freethinker. She had remained at heart a Protestant, and her religious heresies gave all the more offence and scandal, because since the King's illness and operation the French Court had become more and more devout and more and more orthodox. Louis was already preparing for the systematic expulsion of the Protestant element.

IX

Until the end of her life she remained convinced that it was Mme. de Maintenon who was, above all, responsible for her estrangement from the King. Her abhorrence for the Sultana, of the " witch," became a fixed idea and obsession.

Every trait of her character, every strong feeling and passion combined to inspire her with an ineradicable repulsion. The reserve and the discreet manner of the favourite were abhorrent to her impulsive and outspoken disposition. Her pride of birth despised the upstart governess and the widow of a low-class poet and jester. But above all her jealousy could not forgive Madame de Maintenon for having alienated from her the one man she loved and admired.

When we read to-day the " Correspondence " of Liselotte, we receive the impression that " Madame " had only herself to blame, and that Mme. de Maintenon was more sinned against than sinning. It was natural enough that " Madame " should impute the responsibility of all her grievances to the " Widow Scarron." Mme. de Maintenon was supposed to be omnipotent, and therefore it was almost inevitable that she should be made answerable for everything that happened. No doubt the morganatic wife of Louis could not feel any sympathy for the proud German. It would have been too much to expect of her, that she should requite the implacable hatred of " Madame " with kind offices of friendship. But we have no reason to suppose that Mme. de Maintenon went out of her way to do any disservice to the King's sister-in-law. The hatred was all on one side. Secure in the love of the King, Mme. de Maintenon could afford to despise and ignore the passionate outbursts of her implacable and impotent German enemy.

X

Humiliated and persecuted by her husband, estranged from the King, Liselotte found little consolation in her children. She might have derived some satisfaction from her only daughter, who was dutiful and affectionate, but at eighteen years of age she was married to the Duke of Lorraine, and was lost to her mother. The tyranny of etiquette made it impossible for the one to visit the other, except on conditions which were unacceptable to the King's Majesty!

Her only son, the famous and infamous Regent-that-was-to-be, although clever, kind-hearted and respectful, grew up to be as vicious, in another way, as his depraved father. Before he was twenty the corruption of a perverse Court had tainted him to the marrow. But what grieved her even more than the misconduct of the Duke de Chartres was the misalliance which he was prevailed upon to enter into with Mlle. de Blois. That the great-grandson of a

King of England and the grandson of a King of France should agree to marry the bastard daughter of Mme. de Montespan was the crowning humiliation which embittered the remainder of her days.

XI

In 1699 " Monsieur " suddenly died of apoplexy, after a violent fit of anger with his Royal brother, followed by a too copious dinner. " Monsieur " had always overtaxed his truly Royal stomach, which was as characteristic of the Bourbons as the eagle nose, and he fell a victim to his intemperance. The death of her husband reduced Liselotte more than ever to the mercy of Louis. The King, as always, proved generous. Liselotte retained most of the pensions which had been granted to the Duke of Orleans, and as her income was henceforth at her own disposal, instead of being squandered on her husband's favourites, she was now much better off than in the lifetime of her lord and master.

But it was one of the conditions of the King's favours that " Madame " should make peace with Mme. de Maintenon. The proud German Princess had to humiliate herself before the ex-governess. The vindictive woman had to forget and to forgive. The outspoken and impulsive character had to dissemble and to restrain her outbursts of temper. The scene of reconciliation, which has been graphically described by Saint Simon, took place with a liberal display of goodwill on the part of Mme. de Maintenon, and, on the part of Liselotte, with abundant outbursts of repentance and promises for the future. But the reconciliation proved only superficial and ephemeral. Outward forms were observed, but the hatred was more unrelenting than ever, having gathered strength from the public humiliation.

XII

One may wonder, with her biographers, why Liselotte, on the death of "Monsieur," did not retire to Germany, or, as had been provided in her marriage contract, why she did not take advantage of the seclusion and peace of a convent, the favourite retreat and refuge of Royal widows in those religious times. But various reasons made her prefer the solitude of Versailles and St. Cloud. Although not a tender mother, it is possible that she did not want to part from her only son. Moreover, to a heretic like Liselotte, the atmosphere of a convent was uncongenial. Nor did she possess the financial means to keep up her position in Germany, and she was too proud to accept a subordinate place in her native country, after having occupied an exalted position in France. And, finally, she hoped for an imminent change which might bring deliverance from the odious tyranny of the " Sultana." So many ladies had possessed in turn the fickle heart of Louis. Why should not a new favourite arise and take the place of the " Widow Scarron " ? Or why should she not herself be restored to the Royal friendship ? And thus did pride and prejudice, maternal love and human illusion combine to detain her in France, and thus, until the end of her days, she continued to occupy with her dogs her private apartments at Versailles and her palace at St. Cloud.

XIII

For fifteen years she had to wait for the great King to disappear from a scene which he had filled for seventy-two years, having ruled longer than any sovereign of modern times! When the change did come it was too late. No doubt she breathed more freely when her detested rival returned to St. Cyr, and took up once more her natural vocation as a governess, after having been for thirty years the uncrowned Queen of France. But Liselotte sincerely regretted the old King. He had been kind to her in her youth, and she had never ceased to love him. Her son had now become Regent of France, and she herself was now the first lady in the realm. And she would have been more than woman if her vanity had not been flattered under the changed circumstances. On the other hand, she less than ever approved of the ways of her family. Her son was addicted to women and gambling. Her granddaughter, the Duchess of Berry, astonished even a corrupt Court with her continuous scandals. Of real political influence Liselotte had none. The Regent, rather than listen to the counsels of his mother, preferred to follow the advice of the infamous Cardinal du Bois, or of the upstart Edinburgh financier and adventurer, John Law, of Lauriston, who, with his Mississippi schemes, eventually ruined half the nobility of Versailles, and turned Paris into a gambling den.

XIV

And even if Liselotte, after her long years of constraint and humiliation, had been disposed to rejoice in her new position, her capacity of enjoyment was rapidly giving way at the approach of age and illness. Her health had been excellent as long as she had been able to take exercise, but during the last years of Louis' reign disfavour and seclusion, as well as the tyranny of etiquette, had condemned her more and more to a sedentary existence. Her form, which had always been ample, now became every day more massive and unwieldy, and made motion increasingly difficult. Her intellect had lost none of its keenness and activity. Under the freer atmosphere of the Regency, she indulged to the full her natural bent for moralizing and speculating. She corresponded with the greatest philosopher of the age, Leibnitz, and with the rising generation of German thinkers. Whilst Louis XIV had become more and more devout with advancing age and increasing infirmities, Liselotte became more and more a freethinker, and railed more and more against superstition and sacerdotal tyranny. Her undaunted spirit saw the approach of death without terror. Until the end she plied her incisive pen, and continued to entertain her German friends with her interminable epistles. She died at seventy years of age, only preceding her son, the Regent, by one year. She had spent exactly half a century in France. Since she left Heidelberg, in 1672, she had never seen again the smiling hills and vineyards of her native country that she loved so well.

SIR ARTHUR CONAN DOYLE ON THE FRENCH HUGUENOTS

SIR ARTHUR CONAN DOYLE ON THE FRENCH HUGUENOTS[1]

IT might have been better if Sir Arthur Conan Doyle had not republished a cheap edition of the "Refugees." Sir Arthur has a great reputation to lose, and the "Refugees" can add nothing to that reputation. In this historical novel on the expulsion of the Huguenots and the Revocation of the Edict of Nantes, Sir Arthur has not shown that acute sense of reality and that careful attention to fact which have established the fame of "Sherlock Holmes." On the contrary, he has taken unpardonable liberties with history, and indulged in anachronisms which even the most unbridled licence of poetry could not justify. An English novelist writing on French history may presume a great deal on the ignorance of his readers, but treating of a period which is so near to us and so familiar, Sir Arthur has really presumed too much. I do not know of another novel where history is so grossly distorted and where chronology is so grotesquely trifled with.

[1] Sir A. C. Doyle, "The Refugees." Nelson, 7d.

THE FRENCH HUGUENOTS 139

In the year of grace 1685, when the events narrated in the " Refugees " unfold themselves, the Duke of Saint Simon could not have aired his views on Versailles politics, as the great *Mémoire* writer was only a little boy of ten. On the other hand, Corneille could not have moved in Court circles, for he had died in the previous year, a broken old man of eighty, and his last years were passed in poverty and illness and oblivion. Moverover, every French " schoolboy "—I really do mean every *French* schoolboy, not Macaulay's schoolboy—might have told Sir Arthur that the fatal blunder which brought down the wrath of Louis XIV was committed, not by Corneille, but by his rival, Racine.

As Sir Arthur confuses Racine and Corneille (what would we think of an English writer who would write a novel on the age of Shakespeare and who could confuse Shakespeare and Milton ?) he as hopelessly mixes up Fénélon, Bossuet, and Massillon. Courtiers could not have discussed in 1685 the comparative merits of Massillon and Bourdaloue, for Massillon was still an unknown young cleric, and his success as a Court preacher was only achieved about a quarter of a century later. Sir Arthur is guilty of the same anachronism with regard to Fénélon. Fénélon has not yet appeared at Court. Nor is it Fénélon, but Bossuet, who had leanings to Jansenism. For the future Archbishop of Cambrai from the very beginning was a most bitter opponent of the Jansenists, and his heresy of quietism has absolutely nothing to do with the heresy of the grand Arnauld.

The character sketch which Sir Arthur gives us of Louis XIV very much resembles a caricature. Sir Arthur has learned from the "Mémoires" of Saint Simon that Louis was very ignorant, and I dare say that the illustration he gives is not improbable. The great King is quite as likely to have confused Darius and Alexander as the novelist himself has confused Corneille and Racine, and the Sovereign was more excusable than the writer. But it is most unlikely that the "Roi-Soleil" should have condescended to a conversation with Corneille on such a slippery subject, even if Corneille had been still alive.

With regard to Mme. de Maintenon, Sir Arthur has been kept straight by the admirable Essay of Doellinger, which, fortunately for the novelist, is not quite as stiff reading as the twenty volumes of Saint Simon. But here, again, how little does the author seem to have understood his heroine, and how ludicrous and psychologically impossible is the love scene on page 88! And here, again, he might have remembered that in 1685 Louis was forty-seven, while Mme. de Maintenon was fifty. Sir Arthur makes the proud Majesty of forty-seven speak to the stately widow of fifty even as a lovesick swain of twenty might speak to a girl of eighteen. He makes Louis ask in a sentimental outbrust whether, forsooth, he, the King, was the widow's first love. Even Sir Arthur cannot fail to see that for Louis XIV and Mme. de Maintenon the age of passion had passed, and that what drew Louis XIV to Mme. de Maintenon, and what kept the once so fickle lover faithful for thirty years to the widow of Scarron, was not passion, but the moral influence and spiritual magnetism of one of the most extraordinary women of French history.

I am only dwelling on a few of the more glaring errors. There are hundreds of them. Sir Arthur derives most of his information from Saint Simon, but he has read the immortal memoir-writer with an absent-minded eye and to very little purpose. The expulsion of Arnauld took place in 1656, thirty years before the period of the "Refugees." Neither the insolence of Pascal nor the last comedy of Molière could have been the topic of the day, for the "Provinciales" of Pascal and the last comedy of Molière appeared an entire generation before. The faithful servant Nanon was not young, but old. It was not Fagon, but Daquin, who was first physician to his Majesty. Louis XIV rose at eight in the morning, and not at eight-thirty. Louis XIV did not wholly depend on his *valets de chambre* in the ritual of dress, and he performed it himself with becoming grace and majesty, as Saint Simon is careful to add. Louis XIV was never lax in the discharge of his religious duties, and he only once missed attending Mass, and that only in the course of a strenuous campaign. It is Louvois, and not Colbert, who created the Invalides. The famous scene of the window of Trianon occurred at a later date, and was, according to Saint Simon, the futile cause of the European War of 1688. Louis XIV threatened Louvois with pincers, not because he had sent a letter to Lord Sunderland, but because he had ordered the archiepiscopal and electoral city of Treves to be burnt. The Marquis de Montespan only died in 1700. Bontemps could not have called Mme. de Maintenon the " new one," for she had been at Court for ten years, and a favourite for five.

The writer who perpetrates such glaring mistakes in matters of detail is not likely to be more trustworthy with regard to the main subject

THE FRENCH HUGUENOTS 143

and purpose of his book. According to Sir Arthur, the Revocation of the Edict of Nantes was the result of a fiendish plot between Bossuet, the Jesuit Confessor, and Mme. de Maintenon. Mme. de Maintenon pledged herself to use her influence over Louis XIV in order to secure the expulsion of her former co-religionists, and the Churchmen pledged themselves to use their influence to bring about her marriage with the King. So intimate is the connection between one event and the other that in the novel the Revocation takes place two days after the marriage, whereas, in point of fact, the marriage took place in December, 1684, and the Revocation was signed in October, 1685. No doubt the combination of Love and Fanaticism is very melodramatic. Unfortunately, it is absolutely untrue to history. The expulsion of the Huguenots would have occurred without Mme. de Maintenon, and without the Jesuit Father, La Chaise. So far from encouraging the marriage with Louis XIV, Father La Chaise resolutely opposed it.

No act of Louis XIV has been more generally approved of by his contemporaries than the Revocation. It is not only a big-hearted woman like Mme. de Maintenon, or a gentle prelate like Fénélon, who gave their assent. Even the persecuted Jansenists demanded the expulsion of the Huguenots, even as the saintly Gerson demanded the condemnation of John Huss.

The whole French nation, therefore, are responsible for the deed, and it is grossly unfair, and it is only humouring popular ignorance and popular prejudice, to single out one woman and a bishop and a Jesuit, and make them the scapegoats of a national policy. And what is even more relevant to our general criticism, it is entirely to misrepresent that great historical tragedy, to narrate which was, after all, the main purpose of the author of the "Refugees."

ROUSSEAU'S "ÉMILE"

ROUSSEAU'S ÉMILE

I

ROUSSEAU'S "Émile" is one of the strangest paradoxes of the whole history of literature. It is a book composed by a man in the grip of a fatal mental disease, yet it is one of the sanest and wisest books ever written on the conduct of life. It is the work of a Bohemian and a vagabond who had sent his own children to a foundling hospital, yet it remains to this day the most stimulating and the most inspiring treatise on the theory and practice of education. It is the utterance of the last consistent Protestant, of the greatest of the children of Calvin, who, unlike modern Protestants, protested all his life, and yet it is a work essentially catholic and universal.

On its publication in 1762, the powers, temporal and spiritual, took sudden alarm. "Émile" was burnt by order of Parliament. It was condemned in a special charge by the Archbishop of Paris, and the author narrowly escaped imprisonment, and had only just time to seek refuge in his native Switzerland. And Church and State had good reason to be alarmed, for no single book did more to overthrow the old monarchy and to hasten on the advent of the French Revolution. Its influence was immediate, it was universal, and it was permanent. Educational topics became the fashion. Mothers awakened to a sense of their responsibilities; aristocratic ladies deserted their salons for the nursery, and interrupted their receptions to suckle their babies. Rousseau advocated a return to nature, and a return to the country, and lo! the upper classes left Versailles and Paris for a simple life of rural pursuits. Rousseau recommended that every child should be taught a manual trade, and lo! poor King Louis XIV became a locksmith and Marie Antoinette built herself a dairy-farm in the Petit Trianon. Rousseau preached the creed of the Savoyard priest, and lo! Robespierre made this creed the religion of the State. Wonderful miracle of the literary art, which thus subjected to the magic influence of the same potent mind both the old Aristocracy and the new Democracy which sent that old Aristocracy to the scaffold! And that influence of " Émile " has continued down to our own times. A hundred and fifty years have not exhausted its fecundity. Wherever there has been an educational revival in the nineteenth century, we can trace it directly or indirectly to a study of Rousseau. Some years ago, in a remote village of the Russian plain, Tolstoy confessed to the writer of these lines that it was Rousseau who first started him on his career as a social reformer.

II

The first quality which strikes us in " Émile " is its lofty idealism. No teacher who reads the book—and it ought to be in the hands of every instructor of youth—will enter on his calling with a light heart. Few thinkers have done more to make us realize the formidable responsibilities which are attached to the noblest of professions, for that profession demands not merely intellectual ability, but the sacrifice and dedication and surrender of the whole man. What Rousseau expects of a teacher is not a knowledge of books, but a knowledge of the child. Rousseau is no doctrinaire; he would laugh at our endless pedantic arguments on the exact methods and subjects which are best suited for children. All subjects are bad in the hands of incompetent teachers, and the value

JEAN JACQUES ROUSSEAU, NATUS 1712, OBIIT 1778.

of even the best methods almost entirely depends on the value of the teacher. Whatever subjects or methods may be adopted, the condition of success is that a teacher shall study and respect the individuality of his pupil, that he shall draw out the powers latent and dormant in the juvenile soul.

III

The lofty idealism of Rousseau is combined with the most minute realism. It is precisely because Rousseau possesses such high aims that his teaching is so concrete and so scientific, for it is obvious that such a concrete knowledge can only be gained through sympathy and imagination. To a mere pedant, however learned, the soul of a child will never yield its secrets. " Émile " has been called the Romance of Education, and it must be confessed that it is often a wild and Utopian romance, but this does not prevent the book itself from being intensely true. Its imaginary characters, Emile, Sophie, and the Savoyard priest, are only an ingenious but necessary device which gives point to the treatment of educational problems. Most writers on education are content to give us an abstract argument. On the contrary, Rousseau is always definite. He does not only say what is to be done, but how it is to be done. He likes to dramatize his lessons. He does not evade any difficulties. He condescends to the humblest and the most minute details of infant hygiene and diet and clothing. We hear a great deal to-day about child-study, and about the application of psychology to education, but how insignificant is the amount which we have added to the pioneer work of the Genevese thinker. With all our much-vaunted methods, specialists will still find more valuable suggestions and observations in "Émile" than in the vast majority of treatises of our modern pedagogues.

IV

With all this wealth of detail, Rousseau never loses sight of general laws and principles, and the most important of those laws is the law of mental development. Rousseau has anticipated by a hundred years the theory of evolution in its relation to the education of children. He is never tired of reminding us that education must not only vary with every child, but it must be adapted to every stage of childhood. The whole plan and scheme of the book is based on a scheme of "progressive" training: first the education of the senses, then the education of the intellect, then the education of the feelings, to culminate in the education of religion and citizenship. For the sake of method and exposition, Rousseau may have driven too far a division of those processes which in real life are not successive but simultaneous. Like every discoverer of an important truth, Rousseau may have made too much of his discovery, but he is undoubtedly right in his general contention that education must be considered as a succession of processes, as a gradual unfolding of several activities, and that the higher activities must be built up on a secure foundation of the lower. Even to-day there would be fewer failures in our schools if teachers did more carefully keep in mind that great principle of progressive education. We would not then see, as I have recently seen, the " Georgics " of Virgil—a treatise on the technique of agriculture—taught in a Scottish school to little boys of thirteen, nor would we see the " Princess " of Tennyson inflicted on boys of fourteen.

V

The fifty pages expounding the " Creed of the Savoyard Curate " (" Profession de Foi du Vicaire Savoyard ") have given rise to more heated controversy than any other work of

Rousseau, except the "Contrat Social." Those pages still remain unsurpassed as a plea for a natural, non-dogmatic, universal religion. All our "New Theologians" are only repeating what Rousseau has said once for all in simple, rhythmic, impassioned prose. The developments on the Existence of God, on the Immortality of the Soul, on the Still Small Voice of Conscience, on the Virtue of Toleration, on the Majesty of the Gospel, are as fresh and impressive to-day as when they were published in 1762. It is, therefore, little wonder that the Savoyard Vicar should have had disciples innumerable, in literature as well as in real life. Herder and Lavater, Kant and Fichte, Madame de Staël and Madame Necker, and Jean Paul and Pestalozzi have all been following in the wake of Jean Jacques. The Priest in "Atala" of Chateaubriand, the Country Vicar of Balzac, Jocelyn of Lamartine, the Bishop in Victor Hugo's "Misérables" are all replicas of Rousseau's Ideal Priest.

VI

It is easy to point out the obvious shortcomings of "Émile," nor is it difficult to detect traces of the mental disorder which was so soon to overcloud and finally to overwhelm the noble intellect of the Genevan philosopher. Those who believe in the equality of sexes cannot approve of the training given to Sophie. Those who believe in stern discipline will be severe in their condemnation of a " negative " education, where liberty threatens to degenerate into anarchy. Those who believe that religious education cannot be started too soon will point out the grave danger of postponing it until adolescence. Of course, any educational system which ignores father and mother, and human fellowship, must be highly artificial. " Emile " abounds in psychological errors, but those errors are generally too obvious to be dangerous, and his most conspicuous blunders are only a reaction against the tyranny of the teacher armed with the rod and against the tyranny of the preacher armed with the Shorter Catechism. Even the mistakes of a man of genius and of an enthusiastic reformer are more fruitful than the commonplaces of pedantry. It is only when we strike a balance of the blemishes which everybody can see, and of the inspired truths which Rousseau has been first to proclaim, that we shall realize the value of one of the imperishable monuments of modern literature.

MARIE ANTOINETTE
BEFORE THE REVOLUTION

MARIE ANTOINETTE BEFORE THE REVOLUTION

MR. FRANCIS BICKLEY and Lady Younghusband have added two more volumes to the vast accumulated literature on Marie Antoinette. The French Queen has inspired many a masterpiece, but no one would accord that distinction to these latest biographies. Of Mr. Bickley's little book, the less said the better. As for Lady Younghusband's book, it is uncritical, and makes no attempt to sift the evidence. It is clumsily composed, and makes no pretence of being a coherent narrative. Yet, with all its shortcomings, the volume is full of interesting matter, and the critic almost feels a pang of remorse for having to judge harshly a distinguished author who gives him the welcome opportunity of considering once more the strange and tragic fortunes of the most ill-fated of sovereigns.

I

Marie Antoinette is not only a fascinating subject, she is also a perplexing historical problem. It seems almost impossible to reconcile the character which was given her in her lifetime with the portrait which has been drawn of her after her death. Whilst she ruled she was the best-hated woman of France : hated by the Court, hated by the upper classes, hated by the bourgeoisie, hated by the common people. She was made mainly responsible for most of the evils which befell a distracted country. Her martyrdom was sufficient to transform those almost universal feelings of hatred into almost equally unanimous feelings of sympathy, love, and admiration. She seems to have cast an incantation over every one of her historians. Carlyle becomes almost as rhetorical as Burke. Goncourt, most realistic and most cynical of French novelists, becomes a sentimental idealist as soon as he attempts to portray his heroine. M. de Nolhac, although he sees all her faults, condones them all. Mr. Hilaire Belloc is one of the few recent historians who has escaped the spell of the martyred Queen. He emphasizes her failings, her frivolity, her pride, her selfishness, her indiscretion. But even he refuses to pronounce a verdict, even he pleads the extenuating circumstances of an inexorable destiny. And the " leitmotiv " of Belloc's striking monograph is simply this : Marie Antoinette's life was a succession of mysterious coincidences which fatally led her on to her doom.

II

Born on All Souls' Day, 1755, on the day of the destruction of Lisbon, one of the great catastrophes of history, brought up strictly at the Court of Vienna by a stern mother, the Austrian princess was destined, almost from the cradle, for the most illustrious throne of Christendom. Her marriage was to seal for ever the alliance between France and Austria. It is true that the Habsburg dynasty had been for centuries the enemy of the Bourbon dynasty, but there had arisen since Louis XIV another hereditary enemy far more odious and far more formidable than Austria, namely, England : England which had humiliated French armies in every part of the world ; England which, by the treaty of Paris, had robbed France of her fairest dominions. It was against England that the new alliance was directed. Marie Antoinette arrived in France at fourteen years of age, and was received with universal acclamation. But her very first entrance into Paris was the occasion of a ghastly tragedy. On the Place Louis XV, which was one day to become the Place de la Révolution, and where twenty-three years after the Queen was to ascend the scaffold, one hundred and thirty-two people were trampled to death, and twelve hundred were wounded.

When those tragic festivities came to an end, the child Marie Antoinette found herself transported without transition or preparation in a hotbed of corruption and intrigue. The grandfather of her husband, the sinister old voluptuary, Louis XV, took advantage of the nuptial celebrations to introduce to the Court the latest and most scandalous addition to his harem. The prostitute Du Barry was presented and given a place of honour, and when the innocent Austrian child inquired which was the high Court office to which the strange lady had been appointed, the answer was that her office was to " amuse " his Majesty.

The young girl soon learned the odious truth, and both her pride and her innocence revolted. She refused to recognize Madame Du Barry, and henceforth the whole cabal of the new favourite was up in arms against her. Morally, we must sympathize with the young Princess, but politically her behaviour was an irretrievable blunder. The enmity of the young mistress of the old King was to be the first link in the chain of fatality.

III

The second link in the chain of fatality was the political wisdom of an imperious mother forcing itself on the loyalty and filial piety of her daughter.

For four years Marie Antoinette remained the Princess Royal of France, and both before her accession to the throne and after, she received the constant advice of Maria Theresa. The Austrian Empress sent to Paris the ablest of her diplomats, Count Mercy Argenteau, both as her own confidential agent and as counsellor to her daughter. Mercy Argenteau's correspondence with the mother and the daughter remains to this day the most important historical source and the most valuable human document for the biographer of Marie Antoinette. In any other circumstances the counsels of so capable a mother and of so trustworthy and so acute an adviser would have been an invaluable benefit, but, under the peculiar conditions in which Marie Antoinette was placed at the Court of France, those counsels proved to be one of the causes of her ruin. For the one idea of Maria Theresa was to promote the Austrian policy, which was soon found to be entirely disastrous, and which, as years went by, became more and more odious. What proved even more fatal, to further her purpose Maria Theresa persistently induced her daughter to enter the political arena, for which, by temperament, she was absolutely unfitted.

IV

In 1774, at nineteen years of age, Marie Antoinette was crowned, or, to be more accurate, she ascended the throne. According to the strange anti-feminist French theory, a French Queen could not be crowned or " consecrated." The King alone was anointed with the sacred oil. The King alone was ruler by the grace of God, and the Queen was only his consort.

The whole French nation was eagerly expecting an heir to continue the most august and most ancient dynasty of Europe. The young Queen herself was yearning for the child which was to satisfy her maternal instinct, and which was to consolidate her position in her adoptive country and bring to her the affections of the French people. It was soon discovered that Louis XVI could not make her a mother.

Even the most superficial study of Marie Antoinette's character proves that this circumstance was largely responsible for her subsequent conduct. If from the first Marie Antoinette could have had children, she would probably have become an excellent mother, she would have revealed the domestic virtues characteristic of her race, and she would certainly have avoided the follies which disgraced her early years. As it was, not being absorbed by her maternal duties, and seeking an outlet for her superabundant vitality, she plunged into a vortex of amusements, disregarding every convention and etiquette, flirting with her brother-in-law, Count d'Artois, a notorious debauchee, appearing in the disguise of a domino at promiscuous dances, holding up her husband as a butt to public ridicule, and assisting to discredit the monarchy by her reckless behaviour. Fate would not allow her to become a mother. She became instead a Queen of Fashion, a Queen of the Ballroom, a Queen of Cards, and, in the words of her own brother, Emperor Joseph II, she transformed the palace of Versailles into a gambling den.

V

It was soon discovered that the intervention of science might remove the impediment which prevented Louis XVI from having children. He submitted to an operation, and on December 19th, 1778, Marie Antoinette had her first child. At once she decided to reform her ways. It was observed that the frivolous, vain, reckless pleasure-seeker had become an exemplary mother. But, alas! reform had come too late. The

Queen had irretrievably alienated the sympathies of all classes of the population. Moreover, the reform did not last.

All the old failings of her character soon reappeared on the surface. She became more extravagant than ever. In spite of the desperate state of the national finances, she induced her husband to buy for her the palace of Saint Cloud. She extended the Trianon. She prided herself more than ever on being the queen of fashion, the arbiter of elegance, and she started the most ridiculous vagaries in dress. She paid a thousand francs for a feather. The expenditure for her wardrobe increased from 120,000 francs in 1776 to 252,000 francs in 1785.

She played parts with incredible unconsciousness in a revolutionary comedy, such as "The Mariage de Figaro," which aimed at undermining the Old Régime. Worst of all, she espoused more indiscreetly than ever the interests of Austrian policy, and she caused millions of French money to be sent as an "indemnity" to the Austrian capital.

About 1785 her unpopularity had reached a climax. A sensational and scandalous trial, probably the most fateful political trial of all European modern history, was to bring that unpopularity to a final test. The Diamond

Necklace Case was to be the last link in the chain of fatality, before the final catastrophe of the French Revolution.

VI

For more than a hundred years publicists and historians all over Europe have been busy devising a solution of the Diamond Necklace mystery, and trying to disentangle the conflicting mass of evidence. Recent investigations have illumined most of its dark places. Divested of minor side issues, the Diamond Necklace Case to-day appears very simple, as simple as a classical drama in which all the unities are observed, and where we have mainly to deal with the elemental passions of man.

The *dramatis personæ* are an adventuress and a jeweller, a cardinal and a queen. The adventuress, the Countess de la Motte, is the prime mover in the plot, and she engineers the whole intrigue with diabolical cleverness. The Jew Boehmer, the Cardinal de Rohan, and Marie Antoinette are but tools in her hands. The plot can be summed up in a few lines. On the one hand, the Hebrew jeweller wants to sell a diamond necklace of priceless value. On the other hand, the adventuress wants to appropriate the wonderful prize. It is obvious that, left to her own devices, the Countess de la Motte could never have got possession of the Necklace. She could only secure it through the influence of Cardinal de Rohan, who alone could inspire sufficient confidence in the jeweller, and induce him to part with his treasure. She therefore persuaded the Cardinal that Marie Antoinette eagerly wanted the Necklace, that she dared not buy it openly for fear of public opinion, that she would be grateful if the Cardinal were discreetly to negotiate the purchase, and that this would be the best means of recovering the good graces of the Queen.

The plot succeeds, the Cardinal falls an easy prey, and buys the Necklace on behalf of the Queen. The Necklace is transferred to Countess de la Motte, and disposed of in London by her accomplice. The theft is discovered, and the jeweller, pressing for payment, reveals that an adventuress, surrounded by a band of malefactors, has used the name, impersonated the character, and forged the handwriting of the Queen of France. Louis XVI, in an evil hour, and in an impulse of righteous indignation, decides to avenge the honour of the Queen and the majesty of the throne. The Cardinal is arrested and is brought to trial before the High Court of Parliament. The whole nation takes sides, but it takes sides against Marie Antoinette. The Parliament uses a unique opportunity of humiliating the monarchy. The Church is determined to defend the privileges of the ecclesiastical order. The higher nobility consider it their duty to defend one of their own class. The trial lasts three hundred days, and for three hundred days the Court, the Church, the nobility are dragged in the mud. The adventuress is condemned, but her credulous victim is acquitted. The acquittal of the Cardinal is the condemnation of the Queen.

It has been well said that the Diamond Necklace trial sounded the knell of the old monarchy, that it was the beginning of the French Revolution. And it is now easy to see, in the light of later events, that when the catastrophe did come, Marie Antoinette was bound to be the first victim. The very weakness of her husband and her strength of will were to be turned against her. As it was obvious to all that Louis XVI was but an instrument in her hands, she alone was to be held accountable for all the calamities which befell the monarchy and the nation, she alone was to be made responsible for the opposition to the Revolution and for the armed intervention of Europe.

MIRABEAU

MIRABEAU

MIRABEAU has exercised not only on his contemporaries, but on posterity, an extraordinary fascination.

Certainly, I admit that it is difficult to refrain from admiring this presigeotus and striking personality, but it must also be admitted that it is difficult, judging him simply by the actions of his private and public life, to come to any other conclusion regarding Mirabeau, than that he is one of the most infamous scoundrels in history. One might almost say that of all the legends of the Revolution, there is not one more fabulous, or more legendary, than that of Mirabeau : of a Byronian hero, of a mixture of greatness and meanness, of generous virtues and degrading vices. Indeed, I look in vain for his virtues either public or private ; as for his vices, I see them flaunting themselves everywhere with shameless impudence. In the same way, it would be difficult to name a single vice from which Mirabeau was exempt. Inveterate lying and habitual plagiarism are only venial sins to him. He is hypocritical and mercenary. He is debauched, utterly depraved, an erotomaniac, scandalizing by his orgies even a generation when debauch was the fashion. . . .

Riquetti may or may not be of Italian origin, but in any case he has the worst vices of the Italians of the Renascence, in particular those of duplicity and treachery. Treason is as natural a weapon to him as the dagger to the Neapolitan bandit. He has betrayed every cause, public and private; betraying his father in favour of his mother and his mother in favour of his father—when it was to his interest to be reconciled to the paternal authority; betraying his wife for his mistresses and his mistresses for his wife—when the question of money became pressing; betraying the King in favour of the people and the people in favour of the populace. In his private life, his treason was all the more insidious because he made such a parade of sincerity and frankness. In his public life, his treason was all the more odious because his political principles were invariable. An agent in doubtful transactions, selling successively libraries, ministers and princes, in turn, mean, vile, arrogant, impudent, presumptuous, greeting 1789 as providing an outlet for a miserable career that seemed without an issue, fishing in the troubled waters of revolutions, one might say that his character is nothing but a tissue of vices and his life only a succession of infamies.

Mirabeau has been compared to Milton's Satan. The comparison is certainly flattering to Mirabeau. Cynical, yes, but Satanic never! Milton's Satan is distinguished by nothing so much as his superb pride, and a certain indescribable dignity. The dignity and pride of Mirabeau, on the contrary, are sunk in the wreck of his other virtues, and this strange " Satan " sinks to the level of even begging for orders of arrest to get rid of his creditors, ready to lay the blame of these orders on his father's implacable cruelty.

That there may have been at bottom, in the uttermost depth of this depraved nature, some generous impulses and intentions, noble aspirations, virile resolutions and an indomitable will, all contemporaries agree, and why deny it? Let us by all means, in order to explain why these intentions and generous instincts and impulses have nearly always miscarried; why this indomitable will has ended only in velleities, or, rather, in cowardly deeds and shameful capitulations of conscience, let us, in order to explain this sad drama, this miserable struggle from which Mirabeau always comes out vanquished, let us plead as extenuating circumstances that Mirabeau has been the victim, not only of heredity but also of education and surroundings.

It is only too true that ancestral heredity, education and social influence have all combined to deprave his character and stifle his generous impulses. . . . If ever man were born with vice inherent in him, Mirabeau was that man. His father was an eccentric, debauched, extravagant, and among a thousand other extravagances he was the tormentor of his son. His mother was impulsive, a confirmed gambler, staking her children's fortune on a game of cards! Both father and mother, moreover, spent their lives quarrelling and bringing actions against each other. One brother was a dissolute drunkard, handing down to posterity the symbolical nickname of "*Mirabeau-tonneau.*" One of his sisters was mad, and the other a profligate. To sum up, profligacy, disorder, and divorce are the surroundings which give young Mirabeau his first experience of the moral and social world. All these things, acting on an ardent and terribly precocious temperament—a youth spent among gamblers, low houses and prisons, could only result in a vicious and irremediably corrupted nature.

The social atmosphere also was certainly not

of a kind calculated to counteract the deleterious effects of heredity and education. The end of the eighteenth century provides us with the spectacle of a world in dissolution, a generation where the best impulses are sterile, ending only in an impotent sentimentality, where even the emancipators, the Voltaires, the Rousseaus, and the Diderots, are poisoned with the prevailing corruption and where nothing is more rare than a noble character. It provides us with the spectacle of an aristocracy having no longer the discipline either of war, religion or honour, having moreover ceased to believe even in itself. This aristocracy from which Mirabeau sprang was ripe for catastrophe, so ripe, or, to be more precise, so over-ripe, that it did not even endeavour to defend its rights. They were carried away on a breath of wind, on a wave of enthusiasm, on the fatal August night.

The victim of heredity, of education and environment, it would seem that nothing was more natural, more fatal than the corruption and depravation of Mirabeau, nothing more improbable than the legend of a Mirabeau, great-hearted, and of noble character, and the inspired genius of the Revolution. What has given rise to this legend, what explains the magnetic fascination of the tribune, what explains the indulgence

HONORÉ GABRIEL RIQUETI MIRABEAU, NATUS 1749. OBIIT 1791.

of biographers, and what makes the depravation of Mirabeau so incredible, so extraordinary, so monstrous, is that this moral rottenness is joined to a marvellous mind, and a clear-sighted, well-balanced judgment. The sickening fumes of his orgies have not obscured the clearness of his intelligence : it seems with Mirabeau as if his character and his mind occupied two separate air-tight compartments.

The gangrene that destroyed his moral being did not affect the vitality of a titanic temperament which burned without being consumed. Mirabeau was not content with burning the candle at both ends, but flung it into the flames, and it seems as if there must have been in the tissue of his constitution some incorruptible material, some asbestos that no flame could consume. Nothing could dim the clearness of his vision. Mirabeau, though lacking moral principle, has very definite political principles; one might almost say with M. Faguet that he has a fixed policy, a policy that, of course, he keeps to only when it does not clash with his interests. This man, a slave to shameful dissolute passions, seems predestined to lead men and govern states.

In bringing out the glory of the orator much wrong has been done to the greatness of the statesman. Undoubtedly Mirabeau is the incarnation, the symbol even of political eloquence. I do not know at the same time if the man of action is not greater than the man of words. Whatever may be his gifts as an orator, his fascinating appearance, his leonine head, his vibrating ringing voice,—the literary form of his speeches is artificial and often commonplace; all the tinsel of classic rhetoric is to be found in them; they continually evoke the shades of Marius or Sylla, of Cæsar or Catiline.

On almost every page, metaphors such as the following may be found:—" He climbs to the pinnacle of success supported on the double crutch of famine and paper-money." Moreover, however great may be his eloquence, there are other orators of the Revolution, such as Vergniaud, who might dispute the palm with him. On the other hand, as a statesman, Mirabeau is absolutely unique. Danton himself does not come near him. He has all the qualities which make a great leader of men: definite political opinions, strong political principles, and at the same time, a marvellous flexibility in the means he employs; a genius for handling men, tact, and a sure instinct for those who could serve his ends, a faculty of assimilating immediately the work of others, a faculty all the more precious in that it is joined to an incomparable power of work, an almost prophetic penetration and contempt of formulas; the perception, the intuition even, of the possibilities of the moment—in a word, a far-sighted policy and political methods adapted to the present hour. Above all, we have in him this strange spectacle of a temperament all fire and enthusiasm put to the service of a moderate, prudent, almost doctrinal policy. So great a statesman is he that, if any man could have guided and kept within bounds the French Revolution, Mirabeau would have been that man. No one else of this epoch gives us the same clear feeling that, whatever might be said, nothing was fatal in the Revolution, and that mankind was above the fatality of events.

What destiny reduced this man, this Titan, to almost complete powerlessness ? Mirabeau's impotence is both the shame and the tragedy of his existence; it is the honour of human nature, it is the honour of the Constituent Assembly that it was always distrustful of a Catiline given over to vice and crime. Fascinated, subjugated even by his eloquence, it yet refused to follow him.

This impotence of the tribune has not been sufficiently brought out. Nothing is more false than this idea which appears still in classic manuals that Mirabeau has been the inspirer and the governing influence of the Constituant Assembly. As a matter of fact, he governed nothing. His popularity outside the Assembly was only surpassed by his lack of it in the Assembly. On that point, posterity has been too ready to believe his own bragging: "My head also is a power." A power undoubtedly, but a power more potential than real. On the contrary, we may believe Mirabeau when he himself says that he plays the rôle of Cassandra, always telling truths and predicting misfortune, and never being listened to. Outside the Assembly, his audience too frequently applauded the violence of his rhetoric while rejecting the moderation of his views. In the Assembly, some project was too often rejected simply because it was supported by the Count of Mirabeau. "The Court," a contemporary writes, "saw in him only a demagogue, the nobility a renegade, the majority of the Assembly an unprincipled adventurer with whom it was dangerous and dishonourable to ally itself." And what conclusively proves the discredit that had affected Mirabeau in public opinion is that, in spite of the canvassing and efforts of his friends, he was only called to the dignity of

President of the Assembly three months before his death. Forty-three members had obtained this honour before him.

Mirabeau knew striking triumphs, such as his speech on the Tax on the Revenue, but these triumphs were of short duration. I repeat, when we look into the matter closely, we find he did not direct a single proceeding. He did not carry a single decisive movement against the hostility of his colleagues. He has been in the history of the Revolution only as sounding brass and a tinkling cymbal.

And that is why for posterity he is such a memorable example. This tragic impotence of the most magnetic political genius and the greatest orator of modern times in a generation which certainly did not pride itself on its prudery, contains a great moral lesson : that, when it comes to taking part in the governing of men, the most fascinating and powerful genius cannot with impunity place himself above the most elementary rules of the human conscience. One might be, like Bacon, both a great thinker and a notorious knave ; one might be, like Napoleon, a great soldier and a renowned bandit ; one cannot be, like Mirabeau, both a statesman and a miserable adventurer.

ROBESPIERRE

ROBESPIERRE

I

THE year 1793 stands out as the *Annus Mirabilis* of modern history, the year of wonder and terror, of victories abroad, of massacres at home. During those fateful months, Maximilian Robespierre is the absolute ruler of France until the culminating tragedy of the Ninth of Thermidor, when, with shattered jaw, after sixteen hours of agony, he is dragged to the guillotine where he had sent so many thousands of innocent victims.

There is perhaps no other character who has stood so conspicuously in the limelight of history, and who yet remains so mysterious to the bulk of mankind. There is certainly no other character who raises so many perplexing questions. Amongst those perplexing questions I would submit that there are at least three which any student of the French Revolution ought to answer if he is to understand anything in the Reign of Terror.

1. How is it that a man who is generally

represented as a type of mediocrity, a man without any of those gifts which are necessary to play a conspicuous part, a man without personal attractions, without charm, without the gift of oratory, without originality, without statesmanship, how is it that such a man should have been raised to the pinnacle of power?

2. How is it that a man of generally peaceful and humane disposition, a poet and a man of letters, timid and sentimental, who once resigned his position as a judge because he disapproved of the death penalty, how was such a man transformed into a bloody tyrant? how was he brought to inflict death ruthlessly and indiscriminately upon young girls and old men and pregnant women?

3. And, most difficult of all questions, how is it that the most spirited of Continental nations submitted for two years to an abominable tyranny, which would have spurred into rebellion even Egyptian fellaheen? How is it that the most frivolous and the gayest of European capitals was made to submit to the rule of a gloomy Puritan, whose every word seemed to be a challenge to the national temperament?

An exhaustive answer to those three questions would give us the explanation of the Revolutionary tragedy.

II

The rise of Robespierre to supreme power is at first sight one of the paradoxes of history. All the other actors of the French Revolution possessed at least some outstanding quality which helps us to understand their influence. Robespierre had no such quality. He had none of the titanic power of Mirabeau or Danton. He had none of the wit of Camille Desmoulins. He had none of the oratorical gifts of the ill-fated Girondists. He cannot even lay claim to the cynicism and vituperative power of Marat, nor to the fiendish perversity of Fouché and Talleyrand.

Most historians are agreed that the secret of his power and popularity lies, above all, in his absolute integrity. He was omnipotent because he was supposed to be incorruptible. And the explanation is no doubt true so far as it goes; and it is a memorable lesson in political conduct to all statesmen, present and future. It is a striking commentary on Montesquieu's dictum, that virtue must be the foundation of democracy. Robespierre's rule was the "dictatorship of virtue." In a city where suspicion was rife and where corruption was rampant, here was a man who could be absolutely trusted. In an age of equality, where all superiority of rank and wealth was odious, where to be called an aristocrat meant a sentence of death, here was a man who, although invested with plenary power, continued to live in Spartan simplicity. Mirabeau and Danton, with all their titanic gifts, were distrusted because they were known to be venal. Robespierre, with all his mediocrity, possessed the confidence of the people because even his worst enemies could not suspect him of bribery or corruption.

III

The incorruptibility of Robespierre is certainly one element of the problem, but it is not the whole problem. It explains why the French people trusted him; it does not explain why they believed in him.

The real reason why the Revolutionists believed in Robespierre was that Robespierre believed in the Revolution.

The whole secret of Robespierre's power lies in the mystic region of faith. With all his inhumanity, his pedantry, his egotism, his meanness, his vindictiveness, his cowardice, he had the one great theological virtue of faith—a faith unquestioning and unwavering. And it was his faith and not his works which saved him. When everything was hanging in the balance, when the Revolution was threatened by foes internal and external, the people could turn to the obscure deputy from Arras, firm like a rock, confident of victory, biding his time, challenging danger.

And not only had he faith, but his faith was embodied in a creed, in a doctrine sufficiently vague to attract temperaments the most diverse, sufficiently precise to unite his believers in a common formula. Robespierre is, from first to last, the consistent disciple of Rousseau. He preaches the gospel according to Jean Jacques. The " Social Contract " sums up his political profession. The " Confession of the Savoyard Vicar " sums up his religious creed.

IV

The two explanations just given may account for Robespierre's unlimited influence, but they do not explain the horrors of the Reign of Terror. They do not explain how Robespierre should have become responsible for the most sanguinary tyranny of modern times. That Robespierre was naturally humane cannot be doubted. He had been steeped in the sentimental literature of the times, and his favourite author was the most sentimental of all. He was so sensitive to suffering that, if we are to believe his sister, he, for months, mourned the death of a favourite pigeon. Although he was afraid of the sex, although as much as John Knox he abhorred the regiment of women, he was idolized by the women about him, by his sister, by the wife and daughters of the carpenter Duplay. And although he was no Socialist, although he was a strong believer in the rights of property, he sincerely felt for the people.

He was essentially what we would call to-day a pacifist and a philanthropist. When a war with England was in the balance, he firmly declared for peace. As late as 1791 he made an eloquent speech against the death penalty. Yet this pacifist, this opponent of the death penalty, eventually reduced terror to a principle and made the guillotine an instrument of government.

The only explanation is to be found in Robespierre's fanaticism. He probably illustrates better than any other modern statesman the destructive influence of religious bigotry. There is no temperament which is so completely inimical to all feelings of humanity, which is so invariably brought into play to justify every excess of cruelty. For the religious fanatic, obsessed by his creed, is ever ready to sacrifice every other human consideration to the triumph of his principles. He is ready to pour rivers of innocent blood, he is ready to plunge his country into civil war to secure the domination of his sect. He is ever ready to destroy the body in order to save the soul. Fanaticism may be more or less enlightened, the creed may be more or less beneficent, but, from the moment the religious enthusiast is prepared to employ the power of the State to impose his religion, the result is almost invariably the same.

Robespierre believed that the Revolution was not merely a political upheaval, but that it was a revelation from on high, and that it implied a new religion. His one ambition was to establish on earth the reign of virtue, the Cult of the Supreme Being, the Immortality of the Soul. And he also saw that the establishment of the new Deism was imperilled by powerful enemies abroad and by more relentless enemies at home. He was, therefore, perfectly consistent in insisting that those enemies should be crushed at whatever cost. It was the old argument, and the old metaphor of the surgical operation to be performed on the body. It was necessary to sacrifice the putrescent limb if the whole body politic was to be preserved.

It was necessary to sacrifice a few thousands of atheists and libertines to redeem the millions. Robespierre belongs to the same type as Torquemada and Philip II, as John Knox and Calvin. He is a combination of the Catholic Inquisitor and the Protestant Puritan. He is the most rigid and ruthless of religious bigots.

V

But, granting that Robespierre was a bitter fanatic and that his fanaticism was destructive of his humanity, there still remains to explain how a witty and gifted people, in an age of enlightenment, should have submitted to the despotism of this Puritan Inquisitor; how inside the National Convention 600 deputies were cowed into abject compliance; how outside the Convention a whole people obeyed the oracles of the sinister pedant and pontiff. The problem must be admitted to be a most difficult one, and a thinker who would solve it would explain both the paradox of Robespierre and the paradox of French history.

I would submit that the only possible explanation is to be found in the double strain which runs through the French character. We are too apt to forget that France is not merely the country of wit and epigram, of the *chanson* and the *salon*. Deep down in the national temperament there is a Celtic fervour, a relentless idealism, a religious enthusiasm, a theocratic and fanatic spirit. No one will understand French history who does not realize that the French people are by far the most religious people of modern Europe. It is this religious and theocratic spirit which explains the human sacrifices of the Druids in the ancient forests of Gaul, which explains the Gothic cathedrals and the scholastic philosophy, the Crusades and Joan of Arc. It is this spirit which explains the wars of religion. It is this spirit which explains Calvin—the French father of Swiss and Scottish Presbyterianism. It is the same spirit which explains the expulsion of the Huguenots and the bigotry of the Jansenists.

And my contention is that it is the same spirit which asserts itself in the theocratic experiments of Robespierre, in his Cult of the Supreme Being. The special form which the terror did take, its bloody excesses, the power it gave to a handful of scoundrels, are sufficiently explained by the prevailing anarchy which emptied the prisons of their criminal inmates. It is a mere accident of history, which often repeats itself whenever the social order collapses, and which quite recently repeated itself during the chaos of the Russian Revolution.

But the Reign of Terror itself, apart from the special forms it assumed, is not a mere accident; it was pre-eminently a French phenomenon. It was a necessary revelation of national character. It was one of the periodic outbursts of French religious fanaticism. Of that outburst, of that revelation of the French theocratic spirit, Robespierre will remain for ever the most extraordinary, the most repellent, and the most perplexing illustration.

Disconcerting irony of events! If Robespierre had been born in another age and in another country—say, in Scotland or England—he would have been a harmless and highly respected professor of Dogmatic Theology in a Calvinistic college, or an incorruptible Under-Secretary of State in Mr. Asquith's Cabinet. Being born in the sceptical France of the end of the eighteenth century, in an age which was out of joint, he was destined to become *in sæcula sæculorum*, the incarnation of diabolical cruelty, a monster of iniquity.

THE REAL NAPOLEON

THE REAL NAPOLEON

I

THERE is probably no historical character on whom so much has been written as on Napoleon. The last twenty years especially have witnessed in every country a veritable flood of Napoleonic literature. In France Memoirs of Napoleon sell even better than objectionable novels, and their market is world-wide. Even in England there is an increasing output of Napoleonic books, and the historical schools of our Universities give precedence to the little Corsican over the heroes of national history.

Amongst the innumerable volumes which have thus been added to that Napoleonic literature one book stands out as having completely changed our view of the Emperor's personality. I am referring to the masterpiece of Monsieur Arthur-Levy, " Napoléon Intime." " Napoléon Intime " is the work of a distinguished business man, and not of a professional historian, and for a long time professional and academic historians have tried to ignore it.

But its conclusions have gradually made their way, and are to-day more and more generally accepted by those best qualified to judge. Quite recently the greatest historian of contemporary France, Count Vandal, left on record his appreciation of the unique value of Monsieur Levy's research.

In order to put the character of Napoleon in an entirely different light, all that the author has had to do has been to study his hero, not in his public activities, but in his private life, in his home surroundings, in his capacity as a son and a husband, as a brother and a friend. We are often told that the private life of a great man does not concern us, and English historians do not like to pry into the intimacy of their national heroes. For instance, the historians of Wellington in their voluminous biographies carefully refrain from telling us anything of the love affairs of the Iron Duke. On the other hand, French historians instinctively have always shown much less reticence. They have always felt that it is the private man that gives the key to the public man. Monsieur Arthur-Levy has proved once more that the French instinct is a right one, at least from the point of view of historical truth, and that, so far as Napoleon is concerned, whereas the soldier and

Emperor is only an actor playing a part on the stage of universal history, his real personality and humanity are revealed to us in his love letters, in his domestic correspondence, in the intimacy of his home life.

II

The main conclusion of Monsieur Arthur-Levy may be summed up in the one contention that the truth about Napoleon's character is exactly the reverse of the truth which hitherto has been universally accepted.

It is universally assumed that Napoleon was, above all, a man of blood and iron, that the intellectual side of his nature and his formidable will power had been developed at the expense of all human feeling. Monsieur Levy, on the contrary, conclusively proves that the emotional side of Napoleon's character was as strongly developed as the intellectual, that the tender passions were as active and intense as the manly passions, and that as a lover Napoleon might almost be described as a sentimentalist.

Again, it is the universal opinion that Napoleon was a kind of miracle, a "monstrum" in the Latin sense, and a "Superman" in the Nietzschean sense; that he was a savage

Corsican whom circumstances brought to rule over a civilized community : in one word, that he was not normal, but abnormal. Monsieur Levy, on the contrary, proves that Napoleon is entirely normal ; that his greatness consists, not in his possessing qualities of which the average man is deprived, but in his possessing, in the highest degree and in their fullness, all the characteristics of the ordinary man.

And, finally, it is the general opinion that Napoleon recognized no rule but his own will ; that he trampled down every law, human and divine; that he was like an elemental force of nature, uncontrolled and unrestrained. Monsieur Arthur-Levy proves that Napoleon was bound by the rules and conventions of commonplace morality ; that he possessed not only the virtues which make the successful business man, hard work, order, method, integrity, but also the domestic and private virtues, integrity, filial piety, loyalty to friends, honesty.

There, according to our author, lies the supreme morality of Napoleon's career. He is not an exception to the law, but he confirms it. He does not challenge morality, but strengthens it. If so prodigious and unique a career can at all be adduced as an example and an illustration to point a lesson, Napoleon can only be adduced by those who believe in the accepted foundations of moral and social life. Napoleon did not take any short cuts to power. He took the royal road. He is not a hero according to the heart of Nietzsche; he is rather a hero of Plutarch. One might almost say he is a hero conforming to the middle-class standard of Mr. Samuel Smiles. He achieved greatness because he was a good son and a loyal friend, an honest, hard-working bourgeois. And he only forfeited greatness when, through the abuse of power, he lost those qualities and virtues which had raised him to the pinnacle. Considered in that light, Napoleon may appear a less epic and a less poetic figure, but he becomes more human, more intelligible, more intensely interesting to the philosopher, because more on a level with eternal human nature.

III

Let us first consider Napoleon in his relation to women. We have had endless books on the love intrigues of the Emperor. We are constantly told of his cynicism, of his brutality, but we have had no single exhaustive study on the one true love story of his life, on his all-

THE REAL NAPOLEON

absorbing passion for Josephine. Yet there are few love stories more fascinating in the annals of human passion. And, by virtue of this one central episode in his life, Napoleon is entitled to rank as one of the great lovers of literature. For, even considered merely as literature, his love letters do take a very high place. They are as eloquent as the Letters of Mademoiselle de Lespinasse, and they have a much more genuine ring. Lockhart, in his biography (in "Everyman's Library"), which, after eighty-five years, remains one of the best summary accounts of Napoleon's career, may object to their "indelicacy," but he forgets that a Southern Corsican temperament and a Revolutionary age were not exactly conducive to reticence and restraint.

Very often in the biography of statesmen and rulers and thinkers we find that Love and ambition are mutually exclusive. Love plays little part in the lives of Lord Bacon, of William Pitt, of Frederick the Great, as it plays no part whatever in the lives of the supreme philosophers, inveterate bachelors, such as Descartes, Spinoza, and Kant. On the contrary, Love has been the one supreme event in Napoleon's youth. In love, I repeat it, Napoleon is a sentimentalist. His passion for Josephine burst out at twenty-six years of age with all the violence of a first love, and for the time being fills his whole nature. His military triumphs are all laid at the feet of the adored. But, alas! that first love was also destined to be the last, and that great romance was also destined to be a great tragedy. For the passion of Napoleon was not requited. The Creole Society woman, the " mondaine " and " demi-mondaine " despised the little, lean, haggard, upstart Corsican. Josephine was not only frivolous and heartless; she is now proved to have been unfaithful almost on the morrow of her marriage. She is primarily answerable for the sad change which took place in Napoleon's attitude to women, and in his attitude to life. He left Italy a naïve enthusiast. He returned from Egypt a disillusioned cynic. He forgave Josephine, as he generally forgave those who wronged him, because magnanimity was part of his nature, but he could not forget her betrayal. The evil done was irreparable. Josephine had inflicted an incurable wound. Henceforth the character of Napoleon is hardened, and is impervious to the softer emotions. Henceforth the epigram which we find in his early Dialogue on Love truly expresses his attitude: " I believe that Love is harmful both to Society and to the individual. I believe that Love does more evil than good " (Yung, " Bonaparte and his Times," page 75).

IV

It is especially in his relations to his mother, his brothers and sisters that Napoleon's character reveals itself. A great deal of irrelevant nonsense has been written about his " Corsican clannishness." It would be more correct to say that he had a Frenchman's sense of what is due to the family. In this repect his letters of 1795 and 1796 are most interesting reading. When he is appointed to the command of Paris, and when his financial difficulties are at an end, his first thought is for those who are near and dear to him. The following extracts from his correspondence, which I take from Mr. Levy's volume, are just the kind of notes which one would expect from an exemplary French bourgeois.

He writes, on October 18th, 1795: " A certain citizen, Billon, who, I am told, is known to you, wishes to marry Paulette; that citizen is without means. I have written to mamma that she must not think of it. I shall make fuller inquiries to-day."

On November 1st : "Lucien is War Commissioner of the army of the Rhine. Louis is staying with me. I think he is writing to you. "Farewell, my dear friend. Give my love to your wife and Désirée."

On November 9th : "*The family* are in need of nothing. I have sent them money, banknotes, etc."

On November 17th : "It is just possible that I may get the *family* to come. Give me a more detailed account of your doings and of those of your wife and Eugénie. The only hardship I feel is that you are far from here and I am deprived of your company."

December 31st : "You ought to have no uneasiness whatever about the *family*. They are abundantly provided with everything. Jérome arrived yesterday with a general (Augereau). I am going to enrol him in a college, where he will be well looked after."

He was a model son, although he never was a favourite with his mother, although she often took his brothers' side, although she never believed in him as the humblest of his soldiers did believe in his star, although even at the Imperial Court she went on saving money against the catastrophe which she was always anticipating. On his father's death—he died prematurely, like Napoleon himself, from the hereditary disease, cancer of the stomach—he was the providence of his relatives. As a young man of nineteen he supported his younger brother Lucien on his meagre lieutenant's pay, and he imposed upon himself the hardest privations.

He not only looked after the material interests of his sisters, trying to establish them in life, but almost before he attained his majority he had assumed full responsibility as head of the family. He showed infinite patience to the vagaries of his sisters, to the absurd demands of his brothers; and he used to say that he had more trouble in ruling his relations than in ruling his Empire. His sisters claimed all the privileges of members of the Imperial family, without accepting any duties or restraints. Pauline behaved like a courtesan, and she shocked even immoral Italy with the scandal of her extravagant *amours*. His brothers claimed the thrones of Europe as their due inheritance, and at the same time they pretended to govern without any regard to the policy of the Empire.

V

It may be objected that although Napoleon may have been exemplary in the narrow circle of the family, it is not proved thereby that he was bound by the rules of ordinary human morality. After all, even monsters like Fouché, Napoleon's Minister of Police, who, as a Terrorist, sent thousands to the guillotine, are often found to practise the domestic virtues. The simple answer to this objection is that Napoleon's obedience to moral rule was not confined to the narrow circle of the home, but that in every other sphere he revealed the commonplace human characteristics. He was equally admirable as a student at college, as a friend, and as a citizen.

To confine ourselves only to two of the elemental virtues, he was supremely generous and magnanimous, and he was unflinchingly honest. He never forgot a benefit conferred, and in his last will, written on the rock of St. Helena, he remembered acts of kindness received in his early years. He again and again forgot and forgave injuries, and he possessed none of the Corsican's traditional vindictiveness. *It was this very generosity which probably proved ultimately fatal to him, which was the cause of his imprisonment and induced him to surrender to the English. Being magnanimous himself, he assumed magnanimity in his enemies.*

VI

But perhaps the most startling quality in young Bonaparte is his almost superhuman honesty. In Italy, when everybody was grabbing round him, he alone kept his hands clean. His financial integrity during the Italian campaign in 1796 and 1797 is truly heroic. He was in supreme command of the Army. He had been given absolute political and diplomatic power. A hundred million francs passed through his hands. In Paris Barras and Fouché were amassing huge fortunes. In Italy every general was guilty of extortion and peculation with the connivance of authority. Napoleon alone would not demean himself, and would not accept any "commissions" or perquisites. He remained rigidly honest, and returned to Paris a poor man. His schemes nearly failed for want of money at the crisis of his career, at a time when every political support had to be bought. Bonaparte may have thought that, after all, honesty was the best policy. He may have remembered that part of the strength of Robespierre was his incorruptibility. But this does not in the slightest degree detract from the credit which is due to his magnificent integrity.

The reader may well ask how it is that this

interpretation of Napoleon's personality is so generally ignored, and why even his admirers so entirely overlook the " bourgeois " side of his character. The simple explanation is that there are two Napoleons, and there is little in common between them. There is the young general and First Magistrate of the Republic, and there is the Emperor. There is the hero who achieved greatness, and there is the ruler who was corrupted by greatness. The character of Bonaparte was very soon destroyed and transformed by the necessities of statecraft, and still more by the use and abuse of despotism, by the poisonous atmosphere of servility and flattery. But surely the true character of the man is his original character. Surely when we want to describe the constitution of an individual we do not take it after it has been ruined by disease; we take it in its strength and power. Similarly, if we want to know the real Napoleon, we must study him in his radiant youth, in the epic years of Italy and Egypt, as he appeared to a dazzled world, the conqueror of Italy, the champion of the Revolution, the restorer of order and liberty. The true Napoleon is the slim, nervous, haggard soldier of **1796**, the young man who saved France, not the obese and self-indulgent despot who oppressed Europe.

NAPOLEON AS A SOCIALIST

NAPOLEON AS A SOCIALIST

I

THE opponents of Socialism are never tired of arguing that Socialism at best is only the dream of impractical idealists, that it has never been tried on a large scale, at least, in modern society, and that wherever it has been tried on a small scale it has either been a lamentable failure or has resulted in practical unrest or periodical revolution. Now, the history of the French people shows that Socialism has been tried by the most realistic, the most practical ruler of modern times, that it has been a magnificent success, and that, so far from having proved a cause of revolution and instability, agrarian Socialism in France has proved a most conservative force, and has raised the most efficient bulwark against revolution.

II

Academic historians keep us in such complete ignorance as to the meaning of the fundamental facts of history that most readers may fail to see that I am referring to the *Testamentary Law of the Code Napoléon,* and they will dismiss with a smile as a Chestertonian paradox the Socialism of a sovereign who created new aristocracies and new dynasties, and who partitioned the thrones of Europe amongst his relatives and his soldiers. Academic historians are so much deceived by watchwords and doctrinaire formulas that it does not occur to them that the *Testamentary Law of the Code Napoléon* is indeed the most daring Socialistic experiment which was ever attempted, as well as the most successful and the most beneficial, and that, therefore, Napoleon is entitled to the claim of being the greatest practical Socialist of all ages. I do not use the word in a vague sense, I use it in its literal technical meaning. The aim of Napoleon has been the establishment of social equality, his method the power of the State, his achievement the abolition of the landed aristocracy, and the division of the soil of France amongst six millions of peasant proprietors. Thiers may write twenty volumes on Napoleon, and ignore that fundamental fact. But poets like Béranger, and novelists like Balzac, have seen further and gone deeper than the bourgeois chronicler of the treatises and campaigns of the Empire, and they have proved once more the truth of the Aristotelian dictum that poetry is truer than history.

They have realized that it is the Socialistic legislation of the *Code Napoléon* which has been the enduring monument of the First Empire. They have revealed to us why Napoleon has remained the idol of the peasantry and of the people, although he sent their sons by hundreds of thousands to the shambles of the battlefield. It is not our present purpose to determine the exact part which Napoleon took in the elaboration of the *Code Civil*. His systematic adversaries see nothing but organized flattery in the " *Procés verbaux* " of the Conseil d'Etat, and they tell us that he gave nothing but his name to the *Code Civil*. Even so, Tolstoy reveals to us that Napoleon did not fight his own battles, perhaps paving the way for the future historian who will take up Archbishop Whately's argument that Napoleon never existed. Without going the length of Lanfrey, temperate critics tell us that, even admitting that Napoleon directed the legislative labours of the Conseil d'Etat, the *Code Civil* has only systematized existing legislation, and embodied the principles and the customs of the ancient monarchy. But to grant all this is not to diminish the historic part of Napoleon, it is only to raise him on a higher pedestal. For, on this theory, Napoleon must be considered not only as the armed soldier of democracy, the executor of the Revolution, or, to use the quaint phraseology of Lord Rosebery, the " scavenger of Europe," he is made the heir to the whole tradition of the French people, and his legislative achievement is the ultimate outcome of French civilization.

III

Whatever credit the monarchy and the revolution may claim in the *Code Civil*, one thing is certain: where the revolution has failed, Napoleon did succeed. The revolutionists, inspired with the Socialistic ideal, deemed, and rightly deemed, that the hereditary aristocracy was the negation of social justice, the mainstay of oppression, the nursery of pauperism and corruption. They argued, and they rightly argued, that every citizen ought to have a stake in the land. Imbued with this conviction, the revolutionary statesmen set themselves to abolish the landed aristocracy with the fervour and logic of their race. The early revolutionists nourished the fond hope that the aristocracy might be abolished by the voluntary sacrifice and renunciation of the privileged classes, but they soon discovered that enthusiasm and self-sacrifice are fitful and short-lived, and that the Night of the Fourth of August, 1789, did not prove to be the night of Pentecost. After the failure of their hopes, the revolutionists soon resorted to the more drastic method of confiscation, and they finally were led to assume that the quickest way of suppressing the aristocracy was to suppress the aristocrats, and to send them to the guillotine. But the event proved that confiscation and wholesale murder were alike ineffective; for confiscation only transferred the land from the legitimate owners to the spoliators, and the hecatombs of the guillotine only transformed the oppressors of yesterday into heroes and martyrs, and only hastened on the Counter-revolution.

Whether Napoleon was the author of the *Code Civil* or whether he was not, he clearly read the signs of the times. He saw that a constructive revolution could only be achieved by law, and only by a law which would be in harmony with the elemental instincts of men, a law which would reconcile the interests of the State and those of the individual, a law which would make no exception of persons, and would not be aimed against individuals, but which would be universal in its operation.

IV

What strikes us most in the Testamentary Legislation of Napoleon is the apparent disproportion between the simplicity of the means and the magnitude of the results. The memorable Article 913 of the Civil Code, which practically compels parents to leave equal portions to all their children, and which absolutely deprives them of the right of disinheriting any, at first sight, seems nothing but a check against the injustice, vanity, and caprice of tyrannical parents; nothing but a moderate compromise between the rights of the older and those of the younger generations; nothing but the extension of an ancient principle, embodied in legislation at all ages and stages of human society.

But if we read the Article 913 in conjunction with the previous, exacting the compulsory sale or "*licitation*" of the family property in case of disagreement, *the Testamentary Law becomes a formidable weapon which must inevitably break up all large landed estates, and make the reestablishment of a landed aristocracy impossible for all times.*

For the Testamentary Law is automatic like a machine, relentless like the guillotine. And the greater an estate, the more surely it will be broken up. The wealthy French merchant may buy a large property and enjoy it during his lifetime, but on his death, in ninety-five cases out of a hundred, the property must needs be divided amongst his children. If the owner did leave it by will to his eldest son, two things might happen. Either the father would have to compensate the other children and leave them equal shares in money, in which case the eldest son, being burdened with an extensive estate with very little capital to work it, would probably not be able to make both ends meet; or the father would favour the eldest son to enable him to work the estate, and he would leave the other children only what the French law compels him to leave them, in which case the younger children would disagree and demand a compulsory sale or " *licitation.*" As a matter of fact, the consequences of any inequality in the settlement are so serious that sentiment and tradition are against it, and, in ninety-nine cases out of a hundred, owners of property do not even take advantage of the not inconsiderable liberty which the *Code Napoléon* leaves them.

V

It has been often contended by opponents of the law, and by none more emphatically than by Leplay in " La Réforme Sociale," and by Balzac in "The Country Doctor," that the Civil Code not only destroys large estates, but also breaks up small estates beyond the point where they can no more support the owner. Such a contention stands self-refuted, even if it were not contradicted by the facts. That the Testamentary Law breaks up land to the extreme limit, and divides it amongst the largest possible number of proprietors, is certainly true ; and that extreme division is claimed by its supporters as the most desirable effect of the law. But beyond the point where the division would cease to be advantageous to the owner and become ruinous to agriculture, the breaking-up process cannot possibly go. Although there may occur individual cases where the minute division renders cultivation difficult or unprofitable, those cases must necessarily be few, and must inevitably be adjusted. Either the owner will ply another trade and work his little plot of land only to eke out his income, or, if his piece of land cannot be worked to advantage, he will sell it to his neighbour. Unless we assume that French peasants are far more stupid than they are habitually assumed to be, and they are generally credited with considerable shrewdness and practical sense, it is absurd to admit that in any settlement they will not make the best possible bargain for themselves.

VI

It ought to be added that, whilst the law breaks up large estates and multiplies small holdings, it does not destroy moderate estates. Country life under the Testamentary Law, and under any law, continues to attract by tens of thousands the city-bred professional or commercial man. No doubt they will not be able, like the retired or successful British merchant, to buy a large estate and raise their social status by claiming admittance into the ranks of the gentry. But they will generally be content to buy a small property, and will do so all the more willingly because its moderate size will probably enable one of their children to retain it. *There is no land on the continent of Europe which is more thickly studded than France with little country houses and delightful summer retreats.*

The Testamentary Law, then, has attained the object which the legislator had in view. The country which boasted of the most ancient and the most brilliant aristocracy of Europe, the country which created the ideal of chivalry, has become the classical land of small holdings. The stately abodes of royalty and the magnificent abbeys of the Church are either picturesque solitudes like Chambord or have been turned into gambling dens like Vizille, or have been bought by aliens like Saint Wandrille and Chenonceaux, or are occupied by life tenants like the majority of the historic chateaux of ancient Gaul. It may be said that all over France real property has been largely transferred from the classes to the masses.

VII

But although the Testamentary Law has completely attained its object, and has led, in one or two generations, *without violence and confiscation*, to the suppression of the landed aristocracy, the much more important question remains to be solved, Was the object a desirable one ? Have the results been beneficial, or have they been detrimental to the welfare of the French people ?

Without entering into theoretical considerations as to the desirability of the object in itself, most economists are satisfied with examining the immediate effects of the revolution. And the main result, the creation of a whole nation of landowners, seems to them so marvellous, so far-reaching, that in the judgment of the majority of economists the testamentary provision of the *Code Napoléon* must appear as the most beneficent law in the history of mankind. John Stuart Mill has changed his opinions on many fundamental problems of economics, politics, and ethics, but he has never changed or wavered in his admiration of peasant proprietorship. And although, strange to say, he has failed to trace peasant proprietorship to its direct cause, and has even, in flagrant contradiction with himself, expressed disapproval of the Napoleonic laws of succession, the chapters on the subject in his " Political Economy " remain as the most eloquent plea in favour of the social conditions of France and Belgium.

But it is only when we examine the indirect results of the system that we can realize all that France owes to the Testamentary Law, and, even though the benefits conferred have been attended with some disadvantages, those are only the price and compensation which mankind has to pay for every permanent blessing conferred upon it.

(1) The creation of peasant proprietorship has enormously increased national prosperity and the productive capacity of the French people, and has proved once more the truth of Arthur Young's aphorism : " The magic of property

transforms a desert into a garden." France has, indeed, become the garden and the market garden of Europe. The vitality of French agriculture has withstood every crisis. French viticulture has emerged triumphant from the dire invasion of the phylloxera, which has cost the French nation more than the German invasion of 1870. It may be that, under the the new conditions of scientific agriculture, large estates are more productive than the small ones; but, after all, political economy is human economy, and it is the breeding of men, and not the breeding of cattle, that matters to a nation.

(2) The Testamentary Law has encouraged thrift and all the prudential virtues. To him that hath shall be given. The man who can buy independence, security, and dignity by converting his savings into a plot of land will be induced to save more. Hence that passion for saving which is mainly the result of the hunger for land. Hence the hidden treasures, the woollen stockings full of louis and napoleons, which have made France one of the great money markets of the world.

(3) By increasing the national prosperity, by encouraging thrift, the Testamentary Law has raised the standard of living. It may be

that the French peasant will submit to hardships which few farm-labourers would submit to in England, but, in the long run, the peasant is rewarded for his toil. No one who knows the French provinces will doubt that, on the whole, the standard of comfort amongst the lower classes is higher in France than in Great Britain, and that where in individual cases it is lower, it is so, not as the result of poverty, but of that sordid miserliness which is the national vice of the French people. The comparison ought not to be made to apply to individual cases or to particular districts. It ought to be made between the five or six millions of French peasant proprietors and the three or four millions of British unskilled labourers and unemployed whom the agricultural or commercial or industrial crises have driven into the slums of our large cities.

(4) And it is because the Testamentary Law has given to millions of French people a stake and an interest in the country that it has made for order and stability. That great constructive measure of reform of the French Revolution has been in effect a great conservative measure. Paris may be the revolutionary centre of Europe, because it is the intellectual centre, and because the French intellect, which is ever

creating new ideas and new ideals, must needs be revolutionary. Paris may be the ever-smouldering volcano, it may be ever experimenting in politics. But the provinces of France are probably the most conservative part of civilized Europe. The French peasant is conservative because he has something to conserve, as the Russian peasant is a rebel because he has everything to gain by insurrection.

(5) Peasant proprietorship has enabled France to escape from the curse of pauperism. And, therefore, without the inexhaustible source of wealth possessed by England, France is, nevertheless, the richer country, because wealth is more equally divided, and because the divison ensures the happiness and comfort of the greater number. There is no corresponding term in the French language to the hideous word slum. The word does not exist because the thing is non-existent. There is a great deal of individual poverty in France, because wherever there are large centres of population there must be poverty, but there is no systematic poverty such as exists in England, and such as Rowntree has revealed to us in comparatively small cities like York. France has been saved through the Testamentary Law from the appalling evil which is the source of most other social evils, and

which must bring about in a few generations the moral degradation and the physiological decline of the British race.

VIII

It remains for us to examine whether those incalculable advantages produced by French peasant proprietorship, which we have just analysed, are not counterbalanced and outweighed by even greater disadvantages.

(1) It has been objected in the first place that a nation may be threatened with an even greater evil than the degradation of the race, namely, its extinction, as the result of the systematic restriction of the population. And it has been contended that in France the Testamentary Law is directly or indirectly responsible for that evil.

Now it is quite true that peasant proprietorship tends to the diminution of the population. But that diminution is in reality caused by a law which is the tragic paradox of human history, and which in all times has been a menace to nations in an advanced state of civilization. It is a universal law and a natural law, which has only been checked by the interposition of

Belgium, in Catholic countries like Canada and Ireland, in Belgium and Germany. In all times and in all countries the increase of population seems to have been in inverse ratio to quality. The more means parents have to support their children, the fewer children they have. It is the proletariat that always have been most prolific; it is the miserable and unhappy that multiply at the expense of the strong.

(2) There is another accusation levelled at the Testamentary Law which is just as true and just as false, according to one's preconceptions, namely, that the Testamentary Law is responsible for the failure of French colonization. France has always produced pioneers and soldiers, but France has not produced colonists, because France does not produce emigrants. But the Frenchman fails to emigrate not because of peasant proprietorship, but because his native country, partly, no doubt, owing to peasant proprietorship, has more attractions than any foreign country. The Frenchman does not emigrate because French life is too easy, and because France is the most beautiful country God ever created, after His own Kingdom of Heaven. And it is as fair to blame the Testamentary Law for the failure of emigration

as it would be to blame the radiance of the sun, or the abundance of the soil, or the smiling vineyards, or the temperament of the people.

(3) There is one other accusation which seems to contain more truth. The Testamentary Law, the small holdings have discouraged industry and checked commercial enterprise. France could not, in any case, not being a great coal and iron producing country, have become a great commercial power, but the Testamentary Law still further discourages industry and hampers commercial development. For, under modern conditions, commerce and industry on a large scale cannot be carried on without considerable enterprise and risk. The French peasant will risk his life, but he will not risk his money, because in risking his money he risks more than his life—he risks the future of his children, his leisure and independence, his place in society.

IX

The above analysis, brief as it is, may suffice to put the problem of the Testamentary Law in its main aspects, and to provide the reader with the necessary elements for forming an independent judgment. In a question of such formidable complexity, raising so many vital issues, where the evil is so often mixed up with the good, it is impossible to expect unanimity of opinion. I shall leave it to the reader to draw his own practical conclusions from the previous pages. For those conclusions must force themselves on his consideration. Assuming that the Testamentary Law has been a blessing to France, the question immediately arises, Why should it not be applicable to England? *It has been applied to Belgium, to Holland, and to many Continental countries.* Bulgaria, which only thirty years ago was living under the aristocratic régime of the Turkish landlord, has become, through the operation of the Napoleonic Law, the peasant's paradise, and this beneficent revolution has taken place in less than a generation. Bulgaria has become, in consequence, the paramount power in the Balkans, whereas Roumania, whose land is appropriated by a needy aristocracy and mortgaged to the Jewish moneylender, has become a feudatory State of Austria and Germany.

The great problem which Napoleon set himself to solve still remains unsolved in this country. Most Radicals are agreed that landed estates are an anachronism and an evil, and that their suppression is desirable. They may be right or they may be wrong, but if they are right they ought to employ the most efficient and the simplest means to bring about the desirable consummation, and they ought to profit by the experience of other nations. Now, the experience of France, as well as of smaller countries like Belgium and Bulgaria, has shown that all other means to suppress large landed estates are makeshifts, or involve such a measure of injustice and violence as renders them impracticable. The ultimate question is, therefore, whether the reform of the Testamentary Law is not even for England the only simple, direct, logical, efficient, practicable and conservative method to bring about a better social order based on equality, and that Mr. Lloyd George can only succeed by following in the footsteps of the first Napoleon.

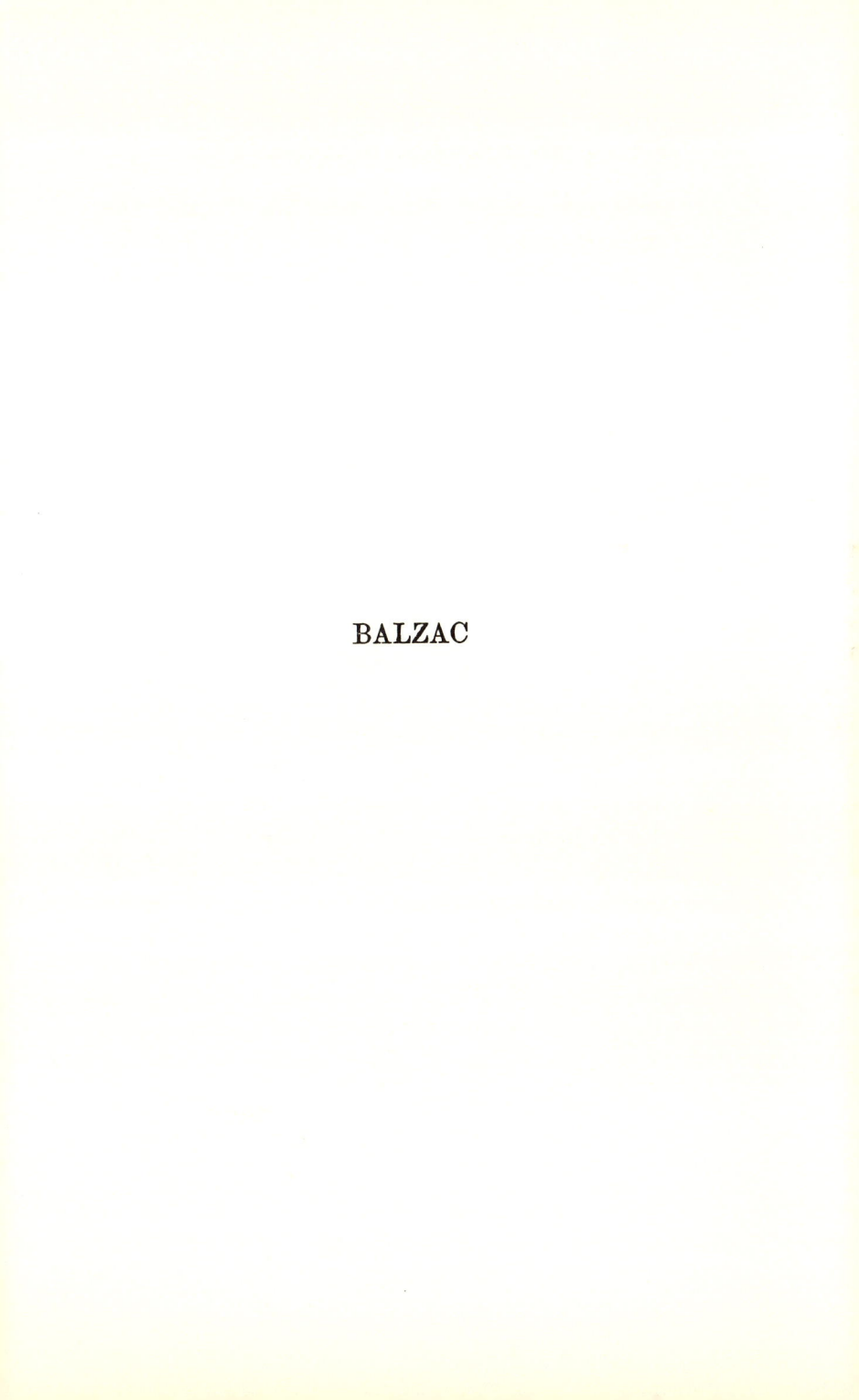

BALZAC

BALZAC

I

WHEN a writer dies at fifty-one, when into this brief span of life he has crowded one hundred-odd volumes, of which at least thirty are masterpieces, when from early youth he has been spending fourteen hours a day bent over his copy and taking stimulants in order to be able to produce more copy, there cannot have been much time left for exciting external adventure. And, as a matter of fact, although there is plenty of adventure in Balzac's novels, there is little enough in the life of the novelist. It is true, on the other hand, that, whatever incident there is, is of supreme importance for the interest of his work. For there never was a great artist, unless it be Tolstoy, whose work was so entirely autobiographical. There never was a writer whose writings bore so unmistakably the imprint of his Titanic personality.

II

Balzac entered Paris like a conqueror, as a young provincial from Touraine, the garden of France, the country of Rabelais. Similarly, most of Balzac's favourite heroes, like Rastignac and Rubempré, came from the province to seek fame and fortune in modern Babylon.

Balzac was a middle-class parvenu, a typical " bourgeois gentilhomme," who wanted to make his way into the nobility, who altered the physiognomy of his baptismal name, and, instead of plain *Monsieur* Balza, called himself Monsieur Honoré de Balzac. Similarly, many of his heroes are endowed with the same high social ambitions and aspirations.

Balzac, like another famous parvenu and novelist, d'Israeli, had many affectations and mannerisms, and those mannerisms are undoubtedly reflected in his laborious style and in the often forced quality of his wit, and one involuntarily thinks of the author penning his love intrigues and his unedifying droll stories clad in a Dominican's white robes.

Balzac had very difficult beginnings, and he had countless novels killed under him. He became a great novelist not by the grace divine of his native genius, but by virtue of his tremendous will power. He was like a great orator born with an impediment in his speech, or like a great composer stricken with deafness. And although those difficulties were heroically encountered, and although his overcoming them must be an inspiration to beginners for all times to come, the initial impediment in his speech remains only too apparent, and even his best work contains many parts unworthy of his genius.

Balzac was constantly involved in money difficulties and legal entanglements. All through life he dreamt of making millions, of exploiting imaginary gold mines, and almost until the end he was harassed by creditors. And the money difficulties and legal entanglements creep up in every novel. High and low finance provide the atmosphere of many a story. Half his characters are either in debt or in the clutches of usurers, or obsessed by their expectations.

Balzac was ever dreaming of marrying an heiress from the nobility, and he eventually realized his dreams. After waiting for twenty years, he secured his prize, and after a few months he died. Even so, Balzac's heroes, Rastignac, and Rubempré, and young Grandet, are pursuing the same quest, and " un beau mariage " —a fine marriage—is one of the mainsprings of the Balzacian novel.

III

English writers, even the greatest, live in constant terror of their special public ; they are in awe of the circulating library. And, like their public, they are afraid of the truth; they are afraid that it may be found too depressing; they are afraid that it may be found sordid; most of all, they are afraid that it may be found immoral. Balzac has no such ignoble terror, for he does not write for the circulating library. Indeed, although weighed down by a crushing burden of debt, he never thinks of his reader. He has a Frenchman's instinct for sincerity and intellectual integrity. His vision of truth may not be suitable for a schoolgirl, but he does not write for the schoolgirl. His stories may not be palatable to the weakly sentimentalist, but he does not write for the sentimentalist. He only writes for those who have an insatiable curiosity for and sympathy with suffering and struggling humanity. He only writes for those who want to be spectators and partakers of the whole "human comedy," who want to be lifted above their narrow little world, to be plunged into the whirlpool and "maelstrom" of human endeavour and human passion.

IV

For Balzac is pre-eminently, like Shakespeare, the poet of passion, of elemental and primordial passion. And, like Shakespeare, he is the anatomist of the soul. And, like every drama of the English poet, so every novel of the Frenchman is the story of one absorbing desire, overmastering, uncontrolled, and spreading havoc and devastation because it is uncontrolled. "Cousin Pons" is the tragedy of the artist and idealist in conflict with the realities of a sordid world. "Cousine Bette" is the tragedy of lust. The "Quest of the Absolute" is the tragedy of scientific curiosity. "Eugénie Grandet" is the tragedy of avarice. "The Greatness and Decline of Cesar Birotteau" is the tragedy of bourgeois vanity. "A Bachelor's Establishment" is the tragedy of the soldier who is unfitted by his military career for the duties of civic life. "Old Goriot" is the tragedy of paternal love, and last, not least, the "Wild Ass's Skin" sums up in one striking philosophical symbol the whole tragedy of human destiny.

V

Most great novelists have their limitations, and only give us some aspects of the moral and social world. They are London cockneys like Dickens, or Belgravians and Mayfairers like

HONORÉ DE BALZAC, NATUS 1799, OBIIT 1850

Thackeray. Or they only give us the Cathedral town like Trollope, or the Five Towns like Arnold Bennett, or the annals of the country house like Jane Austen, or the Annals of the Parish. Balzac has no such limitations. He is neither metropolitan, nor urban, nor suburban, nor rural. He is never parochial. He is ever universal. He may have his predilections; he may love to describe Napoleonic veterans ("Colonel Chabert," "Médecin de Campagne") because he is a worshipper of Napoleon, and because he himself claims to be the Napoleon of literature. He may love to describe priests because, if not in the practice of his life, at least in theory, he is a good Catholic, and because, like every good Frenchman, he has a horror of sect and schism. But he is restricted to no class. If his types of the soldier and priest are admirable, his peasants and bourgeois are equally strong, or his artists and politicians, or his costermongers or prostitutes, or his lawyers and money-lenders. Myriads of characters move in the vast world of the "Human Comedy," whether the part they play be insignificant or important; whether they belong to high life or low life, they are described with the same zest, with the same loving minuteness of the craftsman.

VI

There is one striking peculiarity and contradiction in Balzac's art: whilst his horizon is infinite, his canvas is generally small. He almost invariably prefers the Dutch manner to the largeness and amplitude of the Italian masters. Condensation of matter is one of his most constant characteristics. Few of his novels have more than 400 pages, and again and again the tragedy is condensed into thirty or forty pages. And the quantity is often in inverse ratio to the quality. Even Balzac has done nothing greater than the "Maranas" or "Colonel Chabert," or the "Commissioner in Lunacy"—unless it be the "Curé de Tours." I remember Maeterlinck telling me one day that he considers that little masterpiece the supreme achievement of the novelist, and I feel very much disposed to agree with him. In the good old days of the 31s. 6d. novel, English writers, for commercial reasons, were compelled to thin out and to spin out their story, and to solve the difficult problem of expanding one volume into three. Balzac, on the contrary, is generally more inclined to crowd three novels into one. "Old Goriot" is an excellent illustration of the tendency. In this one masterpiece there is material for four novels. First there is a detective story in the adventures of Vautrin—the original of "Jean Valjean." Secondly, there is a romantic autobiography in the rise of M. de Rastignac. Thirdly, there is a society novel and a "Vanity Fair" in the intrigues of Madame de Beauseant and the Baronne de Nucongen, and, finally, there is the King Lear tragedy of the old Goriot deserted by the daughter to whom he has sacrificed everything.

VII

I admit that this instinct for condensation often leads to overcrowding, and, in the words of Henry James, makes Balzac's novels "very difficult reading." A study of the French master requires strenuous discipline, and is in itself an education. Even as the reader of the silly and flimsy circulating library novel has his taste spoiled for the great Frenchman, so conversely the habitual reading of Balzac spoils one for the circulating library.

But in many of his novels Balzac has avoided the danger of overcrowding the canvas, and, instead of following the diverse fortunes of several characters, concentrates on one single subject. This applies, of course, to all his short stories, but even some of his greater novels are nothing but the isolated study of a single French family represented by three or four characters. In this connection no critic seems to have noticed that " Eugénie Grandet," the " Quest of the Absolute," the " Greatness and Decline of Cesar Birotteau," are all cast in the same mould, and that they are all equally classical in their severe restraint, in their strict observance of the unities. Those three domestic dramas in their structure and composition present striking analogies with the domestic comedies of Molière. Even as in " L'Avare," in " Les Femmes Savants," in " Le Malade Imaginaire," we are presented with the comic picture of the typical French home, so we are given here a tragic picture. And in each comedy and in each novel the analogy extends even to the presence of the inevitable and irrepressible domestic servant.

VIII

It is interesting to note that in the case of the three masterpieces just mentioned, it is the woman who is the nobler character. Ruskin tells us in his " Sesame and Lilies " that in Shakespeare's tragedies it is almost invariably the woman who has to suffer for or to atone for the guilt or the selfishness or the stupidity of the man. What Ruskin says of Shakespeare may be as fittingly applied to Balzac. And this is one further point of resemblance between the two great poets. An implacable realist, Balzac is ever prone to idealize womanhood.

And this brings us to one of the most disputed controversies in connection with the "Human Comedy." Balzac has again and again been accused of pandering to the lower instincts, and of taking a debased view of human nature. It is the exact reverse which is the truth. The ruffians and scoundrels no doubt abound. But no other poet has created more admirable and more diverse types of human virtue and human heroism. No other writer has higher ideals, although he seldom obtrudes those ideals, although he seldom becomes didactic, except in the "Country Doctor" or the "Village Priest." Those who accuse Balzac of immorality or of pessimism or of cynicism have read him to very little purpose. He is too magnanimous not to believe in human nature. He is too full of exuberant vitality to be a pessimist, and not to believe in life and in the joy of life. And he is too much of the poet and of the artist not to believe in beauty, not to feel the artist's instinct of transfiguring and idealizing reality. It is for that very reason that Balzac will always appeal to those readers who, in a literary masterpiece above all, seek a vision of beauty and a source of energy and an inspiration for a fuller and nobler life.

GUSTAVE FLAUBERT

GUSTAVE FLAUBERT

I

THERE are some writers whose work is greater than themselves. There are others whose personality is greater than their work. Flaubert belongs to the latter category. A Norman by birth, and a citizen of Rouen, like Corneille, Flaubert, by his massive frame, by his truculent and aggressive manner, reminds one of his Norseman ancestors. Of middle-class origin, and being left a competence by his father, for thirty-five years he lived in the country, and this reviler of the bourgeoisie was almost a bourgeois in the method and regularity of his daily existence. The even tenor of his life was only varied by periodical visits to Paris, and by occasional journeys to the South and to the East, journeys always undertaken with a view to collecting material for his literary work. Living, like Charles Lamb, under the periodical menace of a terrible nervous disease, he never married, but his kindness, his generosity, his integrity and loyalty attracted to him a wide circle of friends, and he was loved for the qualities of his heart as much as he was admired for the greatness of his genius. The " Journal " of the Goncourts gives us a delightful picture of Flaubert as the centre of the most famous literary coterie in the last days of the Second Empire ; and it is significant of the position which Flaubert occupied in the estimation of his contemporaries that all the members of this illustrious and heterogeneous group—Ste. Beuve, Renan, Maupassant, Daudet, Zola—agreed in hailing Gustave Flaubert as the master and creator of a new form of French art.

II

Literature has its martyrs, like religion and politics, and Flaubert may be considered pre-eminently as one of the martyrs of the literary craft. A bachelor without a family, an agnostic without a creed, an artist without mundane interests, Flaubert's whole soul was immersed in and sacrificed to his art. Literature was his goddess. For her he lived. No writer ever conceived a higher ideal of his mission. In the service of literature he spent a life of unremitting toil, submitting to what he called the tortures of style—" les affres du style "—polishing every sentence, again and again rewriting every page, spending seven years over "Madame Bovary," thirteen years over "Bouvard et Pécuchet," and spending thirty years between the beginning and the end of the "Temptation of St. Anthony." Under those conditions, it is not to be wondered at that, although Flaubert started writing at seventeen, and although he wrote continually and methodically till the hour of his death, he only managed to publish six volumes in all. But each one of those six volumes is stamped with his genius, and is assured of immortality.

III

He was a strange combination of the romanticist and of the realist. He was brought up on Chateaubriand and Victor Hugo, and for both he professed boundless admiration. He had the romanticist's love of form and colour; he had his exoticism, his haunting sense of beauty, his worship of Art for Art's sake. On the other hand, he had the realist's rigid loyalty to and reverence for truth; he had the habit of scrupulous and minute observation, the hatred of cant and self-delusion. And this double blend of

GUSTAVE FLAUBERT, NATUS 1821, OBIIT 1880.

romanticism and realism is revealed in the dual nature of his work. Nothing could be more unlike "Madame Bovary," which is a commonplace narrative of everyday life, than " Salambo," which is a resplendent resurrection of Carthaginian civilization. Nothing could be less unlike the "Temptation of St. Anthony" than the "Education Sentimentale" or than the striking but disappointing "Bouvard et Pécuchet."

IV

Gustave Flaubert is the spiritual father of the modern French naturalist school. All the novels of Zola and Maupassant, of Daudet and the brothers De Goncourt may be said to proceed from "Madame Bovary" (1857), which has become one of the milestones of French fiction. "Madame Bovary" is the most characteristic, as well as the highest, expression of Flaubert's genius, and is probably, with "Anna Karenina," the greatest novel of world literature. It is the simple life-story of a farmer's daughter who has been educated above her station, and has been imbued with romantic notions. Having only received from that education both a distaste for the humdrum duties of country life, and social ambitions and intellectual aspirations doomed to disappointment, she falls an easy prey to an ill-regulated mind and to ill-disciplined emotions. "Madame Bovary" is the eternal bankruptcy of romance and sentiment in conflict with the hard and sordid facts of real life.

On its appearance "Madame Bovary" created universal sensation, and it is one of the ironies of literary history that its author was prosecuted for immorality by the most immoral generation of modern French history, the generation of the Third Napoleon. French public opinion has moved a long way since those imperial days; but British public opinion still continues to taboo one of the most wonderful productions of French literature. The fact is all the more strange when we remember that "Madame Bovary" is supremely moral and essentially puritan, as moral, indeed, and as puritan as "Anna Karenina," of which it constantly reminds us. Unlike "George Sand" and like "Anna Karenina," "Madame Bovary" does not give us the romance of unlawful passion, but only its tragedy. "Madame Bovary" is no "Dame aux Camélias." A relentless Nemesis attends every deed of the bourgeois heroine, and she is foredoomed to disaster and suicide for breaking the laws of society and of traditional morality.

V

Flaubert owes nothing to adventitious circumstances or to meretricious ornament. We are repelled rather than attracted by the sombre atmosphere of his novels. The author belongs to a generation of shattered ideals, culminating in the disasters of Metz and Sedan. And he is a consistent pessimist. He is far more of a pessimist than the Russian novelists, for in Dostoievsky and Tolstoy through the gloom and the darkness there always pierces the light of love and faith. But in Flaubert no ideal relieves the dreary monotony and mediocrity of existence. No sympathy attaches him to his middle-class heroines. He only sees beauty and grandeur in his art; but the admiration which his art evokes is that evoked by a finished piece of statuary. If it has the beauty of marble, it also has its hardness and frigidity.

It is, therefore, not mainly by virtue of the human truth which they contain, nor by virtue of the human ideals and sympathies which they inspire, that Flaubert's novels will live. Rather will they live by virtue of the supreme excellence of their form. Flaubert's writing is the high-water mark of French style, perfect in rhythm and cadence, perfect in the adaptation of expression to thought. They reveal to the student the possibilities of the French language when handled by a master of the literary craft. Nobody in our generation pays any heed to Flaubert's grandiloquent theories of "Art for Art's sake." Yet Flaubert's reputation has been steadily rising, and will continue to rise, and Flaubert has become to-day, by the consent and admiration of all those who are competent to judge, one of the fixed stars in the empyrean of classic French literature.

MAURICE MAETERLINCK

MAURICE MAETERLINCK

I

To an outside observer the biography of Maeterlinck seems without incident and almost without events. His life flows like a tranquil river with clear and deep waters through a verdant plain. The only events of his external life, in intimate communion with Nature, are the succession of seasons, the annual migrations from town to country, from the North to the South of France. The only events of his intellectual life are the dates of publication of his works, which mark the stages of his literary career like the milestones on a triumphal road. But that even and uniform external life conceals an adventurous inner life, filled with vicissitudes, culminating in crises and sudden catastrophes, in developments and renewals, in revolutions of thought and revelations of love. What an enormous distance between the starting point and the final goal, between the spectral and terrifying world of the " Princess Maleine " and the luminous and joyous visions of " Joyzelle " and " Monna Vanna," from the " Treasure of the Humble" to the "Buried Temple"! And is it not his own personal experience which he has summed up, when he lays down this proposition, which reappears like a "leitmotiv" in the "Treasure of the Humble" and in "Wisdom and Destiny": that the only true human dramas are the dramas of the Soul, and that the least interesting, the most monotonous, the dullest lives, like that of Charlotte Brontë, are often the most intense, those which are richest in movement and passion?

II

A Fleming like de Koster, like Rodenbach, like Verhaeren, like Van Lerberghe, like Eeckhoud, singularly enough like most Belgian writers who use French as the vehicle of their thought, born in 1862, in Ghent, the ancient and glorious and turbulent city of Van Artevelde and Charles V, Maeterlinck always remained loyal to the spirit of his native town, and his greatness, like that of the writers whom I have just mentioned, is precisely due to that loyalty which he has retained to the spirit of his country. He has not, like the Belgian writers of the Walloon provinces, allowed his personality and his originality to be submerged by French or

Belgian influences. He will be in the history of French letters the representative of the Flemish people, the admirable product of the cross fertilization of the Teutonic genius, refined in the Flemish people by centuries of culture. Descended, like Goethe, from an old family of honest burgesses, Maeterlinck owes to his descent a rich inheritance of solid qualities, of practical sense, of ponderation, and that faculty of patient and minute observation which is revealed in " The Life of the Bee " : in one word, all those gifts which have, as it were, ballasted the winged imagination of the poet. And, finally, a Catholic and a pupil of the Jesuits, he owes to his religious education, the preoccupation of what is beyond ratiocination, the metaphysical need, the comprehension of the spiritual life, and of the candid faith of the simple and of the humble, and when in later life he rejected the supernatural, he retained the sense of mystery, and his soul continued to haunt the ruins of Gothic cathedrals.

III

To indulge the wishes of his family, Maeterlinck followed the study of the Law, and eventually became a member of the Ghent Bar. He is even said to have pleaded in the Flemish language the cause of the widow and the orphan. But the pedantry and the formalism of the professors of Ghent University, as he has often confided to the writer of these pages, inspired in him a profound repugnance for jurisprudence, and already on the college benches Maeterlinck turned away from a legal career, with its lucrative prizes, towards the distant and uncertain future of Art and Poetry.

He started in his literary career at the critical and decisive moment when his native country was passing through a complete social and intellectual transformation. In that admirable outburst of talent, which is called "Young Belgium," the first writings of Maeterlinck compelled attention and revealed a new and mysterious force. But it is highly probable that his original and strange genius, both simple and complex, both naïve and subtle, would not have been known outside the esoteric circle of a happy few, and that it could not for a very long time have imposed itself to universal admiration, but for the famous article of Octave Mirbeau, published in the *Figaro* in the month of August, in the year of grace 1890. This article revealed to the world that a new Shakespeare had just appeared in Belgian Gaul.

Hitherto almost unknown, Maeterlinck, at twenty-eight years, owing to that paper of Mirbeau, suddenly became a star of the first magnitude : a memorable example, let it be said in passing, of the influence of literary criticism on the fate of literary masterpieces.

IV

The clarion ring of Mirbeau is like an appeal from literary France to young Belgium. Maeterlinck answers the appeal, and accepts the invitation which is sent to him by France, ever generous and hospitable to genius. He leaves Belgium ; but he leaves it not like a writer uprooted from his native soil, but like an ambassador who continues to represent and to defend abroad the dignity of the country which sends him. Henceforth Maeterlinck will be in France and in the world the plenipotentiary of Belgian letters. Moreover, although he settles in Paris, he will not lose himself, like so many other poets, in the whirl of Parisian life. He will not compromise his originality. He will not allow himself to be turned away from his path either by the flattery of literary circles or by the ridicule of the boulevards. As a dramatist, he will content himself with gather-

MAURICE MAETERLINCK. NATUS 1862.

ing psychological documents, and to study the infinitely diverse stage of life. As a thinker and moralist, he will be content to observe with the detachment of the contemplative mind the most prodigious human agglomeration of our planet. But the observation of the human hive turns him so little away from his habitual occupations that he continues to investigate in his Paris study, in his glass hives, the manners and habits of the City of Bees.

V

The ten years passed in Paris are decisive for the intellectual formation of Maeterlinck, and mark the maturity of his genius. In the full consciousness and possession of his powers, in the radiation of glory which, like dawn, illumines his youth, and soon after, in the burning rays of a great love, his thought expands, his art becomes stronger and more precise, more simple and expressive, and reveals itself in works more and more exquisite, more and more harmonious in form, more and more simple and classical, the marvellous blossom of his fortieth year.

But in the very zenith of his fame, Maeterlinck deserts the capital which acclaims him. Even so the Roman general returned to his plough on the morrow of a victory. For Maeterlinck, more so even than his friend and countryman, Verhaeren, has a horror of the "ville tentaculaire" —the "tentacular" cities—and he has the yearning and the nostalgia for Nature. The artist who has written admirable pages on Silence has fled notoriety and noise with as much eagerness as Victor Hugo sought them. Henceforth Maeterlinck lives in the solitude of the country, propitious to long and deep meditation. In his biennial migrations he follows the sun in his course. At the approach of winter he migrates south with the swallows. With the return of spring he ascends again to the north.

VI

And as if everything were to be pre-established harmony in this so-well-ordained existence, and as if to provide appropriate surroundings for his genius, Maeterlinck divides the year between the Mediæval and Gothic Abbey de Saint Wandrille and the sunny mansion of Grasse. The ruins of St. Wandrille and Grasse, the City of Flowers! Do these names not symbolize, and do not they render visible the two contradictory forms of that complex genius, both romantic and classical?—on the one hand, the feudal ruin, inhabited by ghosts and tragic memories; and, on the other hand, the perfumed hillsides of Pagan Provence.

VII

Thus appears to us in broad outline the life of Maurice Maeterlinck, and the beauty, the simplicity, and the harmony of this life make us surmise that the man is even superior to the writer. No one who has had the privilege of meeting the author of " Wisdom and Destiny " but has been at once conquered by the charm and the moral strength which emanates from his personality, and has been fascinated by the hypnotism of his limpid and steady glance.

The superficial reader who would try to form an image of Maeterlinck from his first drama would probably represent him under the traditional figure of the romantic or decadent poet, pallid and dishevelled, Bohemian and neurotic. It is useless to say that Maeterlinck does not in the least resemble this imaginary portrait. The dramatist who has evoked so many phantoms and visions of terror has nothing about him which is either spectral or transparent, and he does not inspire any terror.

VIII

Physically, Maeterlinck is a solid and almost stolid country gentleman, fond of outdoor sports, a fervent lover of boxing, of the motor-car, and especially of the motor-bicycle. And that idealist poet is, in real life, a man of strict order and almost a business man. To borrow an expression from Nietzsche, he comes nearer to the "Apollonian" than to the "Dionysian" type. He has more affinity with Goethe than with Baudelaire or Verlaine. Like Goethe, he has practised his theories, he has lived his philosophy. He is the wise man who knows how to vanquish and control destiny.

THE CONDEMNATION OF
MAETERLINCK

THE CONDEMNATION OF MAETERLINCK

Dedicated without permission to my friend G. K. Chesterton

I

Roma locuta est. Once more Rome has spoken, and she has spoken, as is her wont, with no uncertain voice. She has condemned the works of Maeterlinck, and she has condemned them one and all. The Belgian writer has thus joined the band of the excommunicate authors who are outside the pale of Orthodox literature—an illustrious band which includes Dante and Milton, Bacon and Montaigne, Hume and Locke, Rousseau and Voltaire, Pascal and Lamennais, Balzac and Renan, Loisy and Laurent. No Catholic parent henceforth shall be allowed to take his children to see the " Blue Bird," or to hear the impassioned music of "Pelléas and Mélisande."

II

If the recent decree of the Holy Congregation of the Index merely meant a solemn declaration that the works of Maeterlinck were neither

CONDEMNATION OF MAETERLINCK

Catholic nor Orthodox, it must be admitted that the measure would be amply justified. It is, indeed, somewhat astonishing that to a large number of Maeterlinck's admirers the condemnation should have come as a surprise, and it is significant that a good many candid Protestants, with that delightful vagueness and comprehensiveness characteristic of our latter-day religion, should have fondly imagined that Maeterlinck is something like a very broad-minded Nonconformist. They conceive that because he is a mystic he must needs be a Christian mystic, that because he has written the "Treasure of the Humble" he must needs be imbued with the humility of St. Francis. In point of fact, Maeterlinck is a humanist, an agnostic, an uncompromising secularist. "Wisdom and Destiny" is the work of a neo-Stoic. The "Life of the Bee" is the work of a naturalist. "Monna Vanna" breathes the spirit of the Italian Renascence. There is hardly a page of the writings of Maeterlinck that can be said to owe its inspiration to Catholicism, unless the haunting obsession of death and the terror of the mysterious and elemental forces of Nature, which give the atmosphere of the earlier plays, may suggest an affinity to the darker side of popular religion.

Certainly in his later works Maeterlinck is at the antipodes of Christianity, more so even than Nietzsche, the anti-Christ. For Nietzsche only attacks Christianity, Maeterlinck ignores it. Nietzsche only hates Christianity, Maeterlinck is indifferent to it; and, in the words of the French moralist, La Bruyère: "Il y a plus loin de l'amour à l'indifférence, que de l'amour à la haine" ("There is a greater distance from love to indifference than from love to hatred").

III

So far, therefore, from its being surprising that the writings of Maeterlinck should have been condemned, the wonder is that the condemnation should have come so late, and that the Holy Congregation of the Index should have waited for twenty long years before putting in operation its once formidable machinery. For twenty long years the works of the Belgian writer have been read in the two hemispheres, and have been accepted as those of a prophet. Honours have been showered upon him. He has received the Nobel Prize, as the most inspired exponent of idealism. Even in his native country, and under a clerical Government, he has been awarded the highest distinctions within the gift of Royalty.

CONDEMNATION OF MAETERLINCK

In Anglo-Saxon and in Teutonic countries hundreds of thousands have assimilated his teaching and preaching, millions have applauded his plays. During all those years his ideas have had time to strike root. Yet under the reign of Pius X, the most mediæval of modern Popes, the Roman censors had hitherto not thought fit to interfere. They had allowed a poisonous doctrine to permeate the mind of a whole generation.

IV

The reason why Rome has delayed so long is probably that, even under Pius X and Cardinal Merry del Val, it has been realized that the Congregation of the Index belongs to a bygone age. In the Middle Ages it might be easy to destroy a few manuscripts. Even at the time when Milton wrote his immortal plea for the freedom of the Press it might be comparatively easy to control the publisher and bookseller. But in the days of the rotary press and the linotype and the halfpenny journal the censorship of books is an arbitrary, dangerous, and generally a futile weapon. It is arbitrary, for even a hardworking Roman Congregation can only select a few hundred out of hundreds of thousands of printed books. It is dangerous, because it is apt to challenge opposition and rebellion. It is futile, because it usually defeats its own ends, and the placing of a book on the Index is often the best way to advertise it and to stimulate its sale.

I do not mean to say that in every case the condemnation of a book has no effect whatsoever. On the contrary, in some Catholic countries, say, in out-of-the-way parts of Belgium and Canada, of Austria and Spain, it is probably as effective to-day as it would have been in the Middle Ages. Quite recently the writer of these lines had an entertaining experience of the terror which the Roman Index still inspires in the mind of the Catholic population of Belgium. A few years ago, on my relinquishing an old château in a Flemish province, a neighbouring farmer in the employment of my family kindly offered to store my books. Last autumn I received an urgent request from the Belgian farmer to have the library immediately removed. The farmer's wife had discovered many suspicious volumes, including the works of Voltaire. She had shown them to Monsieur le Curé. He had told her that on no account should she keep those books in the house. Things had been going wrong in the family and on the farm. A hailstorm had damaged the crops. There had been illness amongst the children. There had been an epidemic among the cattle. And neither Monsieur le Curé nor the farmer's wife had any doubt but that my books were responsible for those domestic visitations and natural calamities. In a frenzy of terror, the farmer's wife decided to burn all the books in her charge, and she would have acted on her decision but for the vigorous interposition of her overlord. It was with a sigh of relief that, a few days ago, I again got possession of my ill-fated library, which had so narrowly escaped an ignominious *auto-da-fé* at the hands of a well-meaning Flemish rustic.

From the above incident it must be obvious that there are still classes where the decrees of the Congregation of the Index continue to be obeyed, but that fact ought not to prejudice our opinion of the wisdom or unwisdom of the Roman policy. For those are not the classes which would be likely to purchase the works of Maeterlinck, or which would be affected one way or the other by the decision of the Roman authorities. Nor ought we to trouble about the effect produced by the decrees of the Index on the minds of non-Catholics or unbelievers. For practical purposes the only class to be considered are the educated Catholics. Now, educated Catholics seem to concern themselves less and less whether a book is placed on the Index or not, and they seem to find in the armoury of Catholic casuists some roundabout way of avoiding the prohibition. French Catholics know, or ought to know, that Montaigne and Balzac are placed on the Index, yet even devout Catholics continue to read the works of Montaigne and Balzac. And one cannot see how they can possibly help themselves. As the "Index Librorum Prohibitorum" includes practically every classic author of French literature, it would be impossible for Catholics to attend school, to pass a public examination, or to receive a degree if they did trouble themselves about ecclesiastic prohibition. The only way out of the difficulty is to consider the Index as a dead letter.

Judging, then, by its *direct* results, the condemnations of the Index seem to be futile. So completely, indeed, are the decrees of the Roman Congregation disregarded that it would hardly be worth while discussing its pronouncements if the mere existence and procedure of the sacred tribunal did not raise some vital issues, if it did not illustrate some of the most objectionable methods of the Roman Curia.

V

For, let there be no misconception, the Roman "Index Librorum Prohibitorum" (I.L.P.!) has little in common with the British censorship of plays. It is far more like that other odious and ominous censorship of books which prevails in Russia. The British censorship is only a ridiculous but innocuous measure of literary sanitation. It is defended in a half-hearted way on the plea of public morality. The Roman censorship is defended on the plea of dogma and faith. The one merely involves a question of police; the other involves questions of vital policy—it involves a fundamental spiritual principle. The Roman censorship is a survival from the days when Church and State were identified, and when the formidable power of the State was used to enforce the decrees of the Church. Rome does not only provide us with her own solution of all problems, human and divine—she forbids us even to consider any other solution. She decrees not only that we shall accept her definition of truth, but that we shall accept it, not as the result of personal inquiry, not as a *conviction*—that is to say, as a victory of truth over error—not as the revelation of our conscience and our reason, but solely on the authority of the Church. Rome insists that truth shall remain primarily external, imposed from outside and from above. There lies the supreme interest of such apparently trivial incidents as the condemnation of Maeterlinck. They come as a timely reminder that the ways of the Roman Curia are not our ways, nor in my opinion the catholic ways, and that spiritual liberty and clerical government still remain contradictory terms. But if the contradiction really exists, ought we not to be grateful to the clerical party, which to-day is supreme at the Vatican, for leaving no ambiguity in a matter which is of such moment to all interested in the religious controversies of our time?

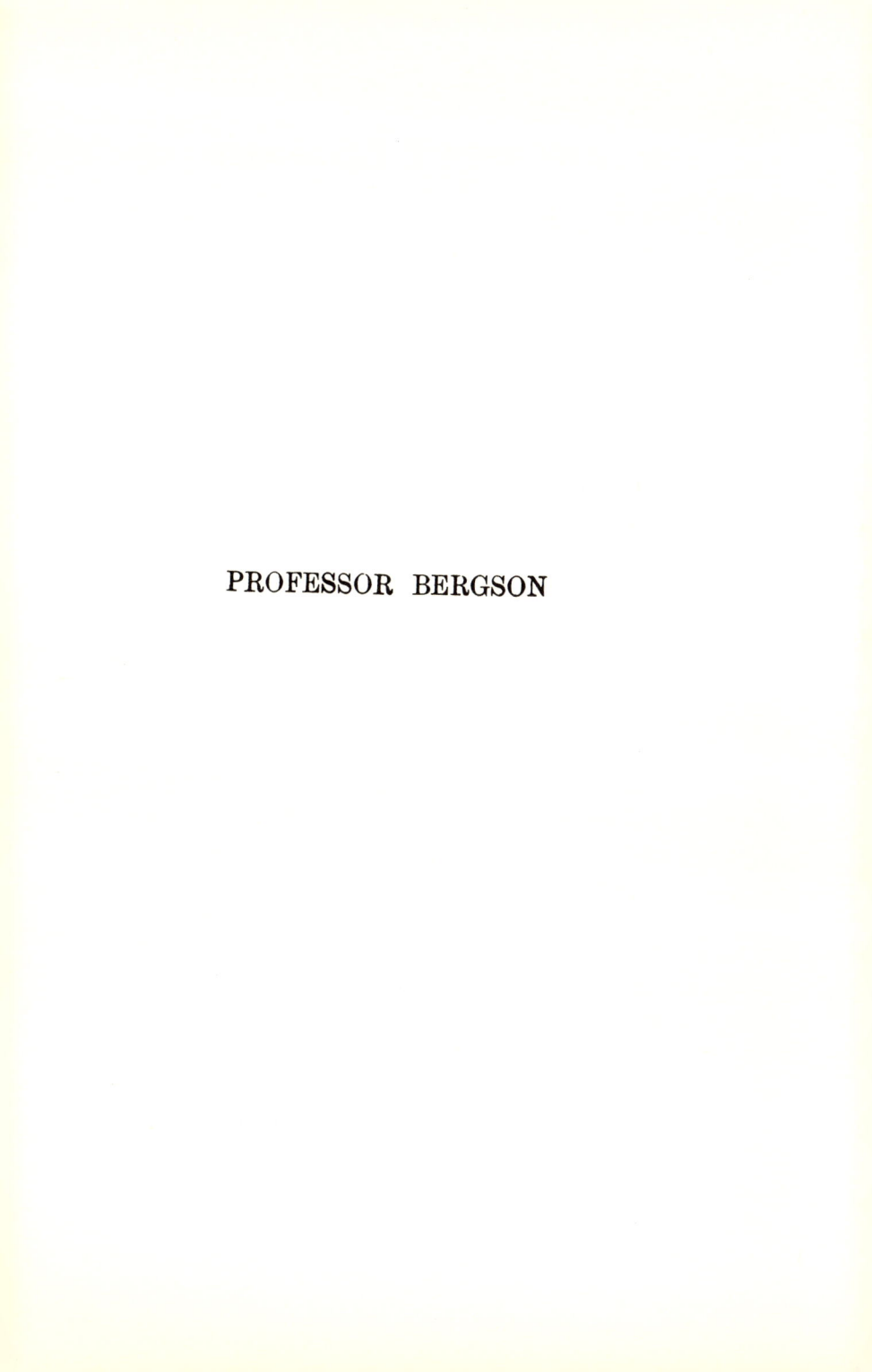

PROFESSOR BERGSON

PROFESSOR BERGSON

I

IN the year of grace 1887, a judge of the Scottish Court of Session, Lord Adam Gifford, left the sum of £80,000 to the four Scottish Universities for the endowment of four Lectureships on Natural Theology, with the explicit object of illustrating the relations between Science and Religion. Those were the days when Science was insolently aggressive, and Religion timidly apologetic; when Religion was summoned on the first day of each month in every popular magazine to appear before the bar of Science; when Huxley and Haeckel, in the name of Darwin, claimed to answer all the riddles of the Universe. Lord Gifford, like Lord Beaconsfield, like Mr. Gladstone, was "on the side of the angels," and he wanted every philosopher to be on the same side. But although he was a profoundly religious man, he was also a consistent Liberal, and he did not presume to hamper in any way the freedom of thought of the philosophers or theologians appointed under his bequest. According to the Trust Deed :

"The lecturers appointed shall be subjected to no test of any kind, and shall not be required to take any oath, or to emit or subscribe any declaration of belief, or to make any promise of any kind ; they may be of any denomination whatever, or of no denomination at all ; they may be of any religion or way of thinking, or, as is sometimes said, they may be of no religion ; or they may be so-called sceptics or agnostics or free-thinkers ; provided only that the ' patrons ' will use diligence to secure that they be able, reverent men, true thinkers, sincere lovers of and earnest inquirers after truth. I wish the lecturers to treat their subjects as a strictly natural science, the only science—that of Infinite Being, without reference to or reliance upon any supposed special, exceptional or so-called miraculous revelation. The lecturers shall be under no restraint whatever in their treatment of their theme. The lectures shall be public and popular—that is, open not only to students of the Universities, but to the whole community, without matriculation."

The Lectureships on Natural Theology, so munificently endowed by Lord Gifford, have now been administered for twenty-five years. It is highly doubtful whether Lord Gifford would have approved of many of the discourses that have been delivered under the auspices of the Gifford Trust, but it must be admitted that his foundation has at least resulted in such masterpieces as James' " Varieties of Religious

Expression," and, generally, in a succession of brilliant and original productions elucidating from every point of view the relations between Science and Theology. That satisfactory result is largely due, no doubt, to the Liberal spirit of the founder. But it is due also to the generous policy of the Scottish Universities. Whereas they might have reserved the magnificent prizes of the Gifford lectureships for British teachers, they have again and again invited representatives from the United States of America, and from the Continent of Europe. They have invited Americans like Royce and William James, Dutchmen like Tiele, Germans like Pfleiderer, Frenchmen like Boutroux, and last, but not least, they have appointed the most original and the most profound thinker of the present generation, Professor Henri Bergson, who inaugurated his course of lectures in the University of Edinburgh in the spring of 1914.

II

Edinburgh University has a glorious philosophical tradition behind her, and generations of students have listened to many a brilliant discourse since the distant days of Hume and Dugald Stewart, when the Scottish metropolis was one of the intellectual capitals of the world.

But no such gathering ever met in an Edinburgh classroom as that which gave so enthusiastic a welcome to Professor Henri Bergson on his first public appearance.

Hard-headed Scottish business men seemed to have suddenly developed an appreciation of the graces of the French language. Frivolous society ladies seemed suddenly to have developed a taste for the study of metaphysics. Under any circumstances it would have been difficult to interest a motley crowd in the fundamentals of philosophy. It was doubly difficult to convey those fundamentals in an alien tongue. To attempt such an achievement seemed an impossible wager. But Professor Bergson won the wager. For the audience actually understood. They certainly behaved as if they did. Not only did they listen with rapt and hushed attention, not forgetting for one moment that they were worshipping at the shrine of philosophy, but they punctuated with restrained applause every passing allusion. They followed with a discreet smile every veiled irony. Altogether it was a memorable occasion. It was a striking testimony, alike to the intellectual qualifications of a Scottish audience, to the genius of a great French thinker, and to the marvellous possibilities of the French language.

III

As one turned one's eyes from the eager crowd in front to the extraordinary little man on the platform, one could not help asking oneself how the lecturer felt about that universal popularity which follows him everywhere with such importunate persistence. Certainly no man ever went less out of his way to invite and to court such popular favour. Almost until he reached maturity, until nearly forty years of age, Professor Bergson was a modest teacher in a secondary school, and every one of the three books which have appeared in the course of a quarter of a century was the outcome of long years of silent and solitary meditation.

And ever since fame has forced him out of his voluntary seclusion, ever since universities and learned societies of both hemispheres have been vying with one another to do him honour, Professer Bergson has seemed even less inclined to sacrifice to the Idols of the Tribe. He makes no appeal to the emotions. There is no attempt at eloquence or rhetoric. Short of stature, of an austere and ascetic countenance, suppressed in his gestures, his success as a teacher owes nothing to the senses. True, his appearance is singularly winning, his voice is musical, and his delivery graceful. His poetic style blossoms out again and again in unexpected metaphors. His eagle eye shines with extraordinary brightness. But the spell of the speaker is entirely the spell of personality. It is the magic of transparent lucidity, of absolute sincerity, of sterling intellectual integrity. Professor Bergson carries conviction to his hearers because a profound conviction animates every one of his words.

IV

Professor Bergson's inaugural address was the first of a systematic course of twenty-two lectures on the " Problem of Personality." It is too soon to define from a bare outline of the first discourse the precise position which the French philosopher will take up, or even to anticipate the general drift of his argument. But those who were already acquainted with the work of the French philosopher had no difficulty in identifying the familiar features of his thought and the peculiarities of his method. One recognized his profound distrust of philosophical systems, of that " mania for unification " which claims to sum up in one sweeping formula all the riddles of the universe. One recognized that sense of the concrete, that " common sense" which is so uncommon amongst metaphysicians, that close grip of actual fact, that caution and philosophical humility which neglects no aspect of reality, which utilizes even the most minute data revealed by external observation and by introspection. One admired that gift for subtle and delicate analysis which is ever bringing to the clear light of day facts buried deep down in the recesses of the inner consciousness. And last, not least, one admired the encyclopædic knowledge which compels every science to contribute her quota to the final solution.

And together with the method and the general characteristics of the thinker, one recognized the original attitude which Bergson takes up with regard to fundamental problems, and the implications which are inseparably associated with his philosophy. One recognized the vigorous protest against a narrow and negative intellectualism which is content simply to deny what it is powerless to explain. One recognized the supremacy of the intuitive processes, the primacy of the will which goes further and deeper than the arbitrary judgments of ratiocination. And above all one recognized the infinite complexity of the Universe, a "pluralistic" Universe of free personalities,

HENRI BERGSON, NATUS 1860.

a Universe not of mechanical forces, nor of regularly recurrent and predictable phenomena, but a Universe ever changing, ever moving, where Time is not an empty mathematical category, where Time is concrete and where Duration is creative, a Universe which does not extend before us in vacant space like a picture, that can be measured in so many inches, or appraised in so many pounds by the valuator, but which can only be appreciated as a creative masterpiece by the æsthetic and intuitive judgment of the artist.

V

There was a fair representation of the Churches amongst the Edinburgh audience, and I am afraid that many a young clerical believer in the new philosophy may have gone away disappointed. And we ought to sympathize with their disappointment. After all, a Gifford lecturer may be expected to throw some light on the relation of philosophy to theology. Hitherto Professor Bergson had carefully refrained from encroaching on the province of the Divine. His three published works are all concerned exclusively with biology, with psychology, and with what the Germans call "Erkentnisslehre." The special interest which attached to the French philosopher's public appearance in Scotland was partly due to the eager expectation that the forthcoming Gifford lectures were going to be associated with an entirely new development of his philosophy.

The anticipations of the public were all the more justified, because, even though Bergson had never crossed the boundaries of theology, he certainly seemed to have cleared the pathway for the theologian. Nor is it the result of any mere vagary of fashion that his doctrines should have been acclaimed by religious thinkers of all countries. All previous metaphysicians moved and revolved in a vicious circle. Bergson broke through that iron circle of mechanism and liberated the human soul from the impotence of scepticism and the depression of determinism. He dethroned intellectual analysis from its proud place, and put intuition in its place. He takes his stand in the very centre of life. Indeed, his philosophy may be best defined a philosophy of life and a philosophy of action. It leaves room for the insertion of human freewill. It acknowledges with the theologian the twin concepts of the creative and the miraculous. Is not life itself a standing miracle? Is not every stage in the process of evolution a creative process, an "élan vital" of inventive genius?

VI

So far, then, the philosophy of Bergson has proved an inspiration to the student of Ethics and of Theology, but it is not necessary for the Bergsonian to travel a long way before he realizes that even to the liberal student of Christian Theology the new philosophy raises as many problems as it solves, and that it bristles with contradictions.

For Bergsonism is pre-eminently the philosophy of Change, of a ceaseless Becoming. Theology is concerned with the Immutable and the Everlasting.

In Bergson's conception Time and Duration are the very web and woof of life. Theology is merged in Eternity.

Bergsonism is the philosophy of Chance, of accidental variations. Creative evolution proceeds by eruptive, explosive vital outbursts. Religion is based on finality. All Christian theology is Teleology.

Bergsonism emphasizes nothing more constantly than diversity. Creative evolution has again and again been deflected on divergent lines. The World of Instinct follows one line of development. The World of Intellect follows another. On the contrary, religion is based on unity and continuity. Revealed religion, supernatural religion, is the deposit of a revelation vouchsafed to mankind once and for all. The God of Christianity is a personal God, transcendent and distinct from His creatures, not diffused in His creation.

Such are some of the difficulties which would no doubt force themselves upon the mind of Professor Bergson's clerical hearers. It is an interesting subject for speculation, whether in his forthcoming course he will address himself to answer those questions, or whether, as he has done in the past, he will stop short of the answer and of the ultimate reality ? Will he refrain from putting the coping-stone to his philosophical structure, or will the problem of personality and its survival after death lead the speaker on to that threshold where philosophy ends and where theology begins and reigns supreme ? The Edinburgh Gifford lectures are giving the French philosopher his opportunity. Is he going to seize it ?

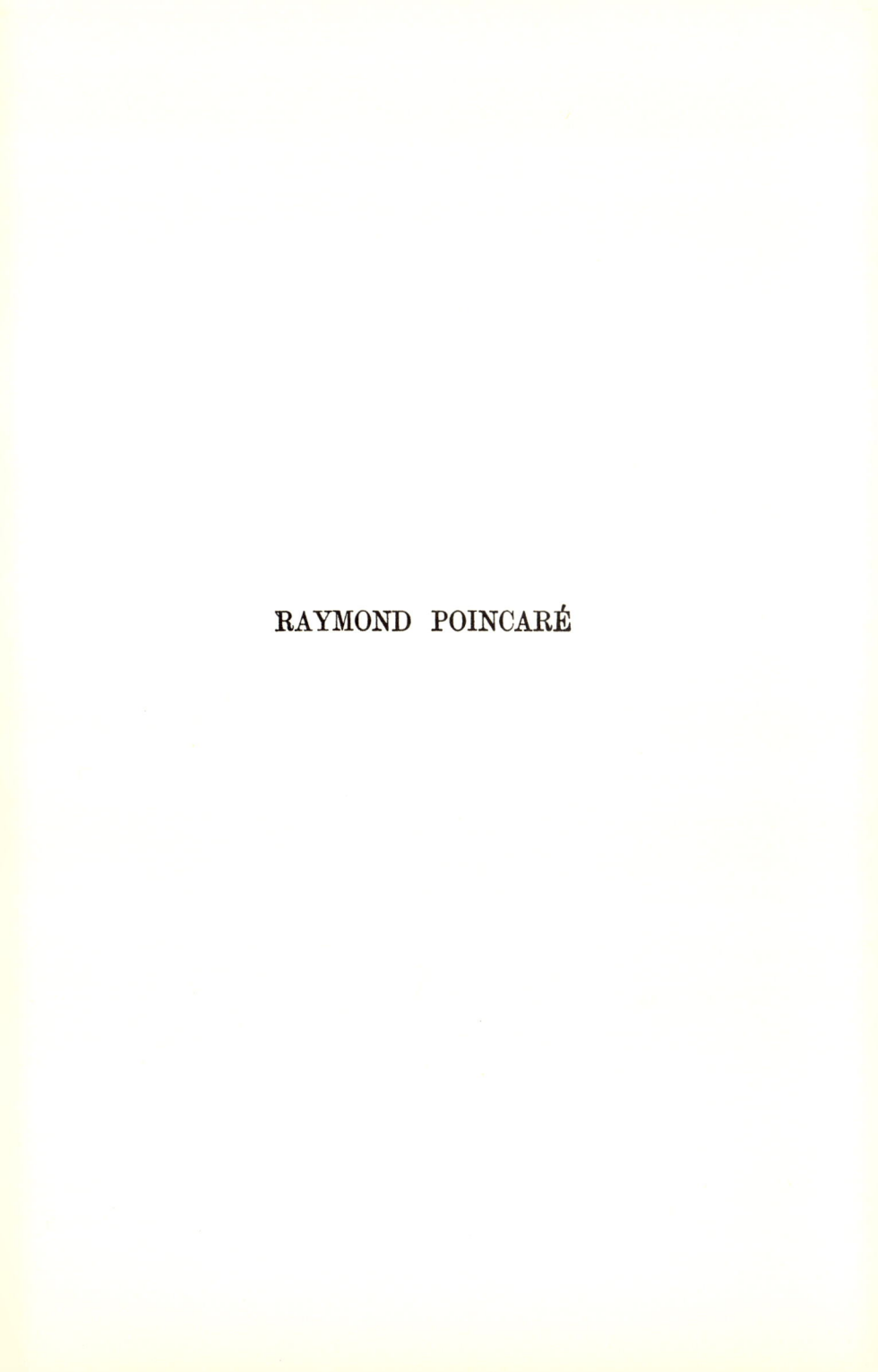

RAYMOND POINCARÉ

RAYMOND POINCARÉ

I

It is often contended that democracy does not care for culture, and that the people have an instinctive distrust for the scholar and the artist. Two recent events are an emphatic refutation of such a contention. Almost simultaneously the two greatest democracies of the world, having to choose the head of the Executive, have deliberately chosen two men of letters: the American Republic selected an eminent University professor; the French Republic selected a member of the French Academy, one of the forty Immortals.

II

I have before me three volumes of the works of the new French President. They are mainly composed of literary essays, of political and forensic speeches. They are distinguished by all those qualities which we are accustomed to associate with the best French writing: lucidity and logic, symmetry and proportion, ready wit and versatility. Whether the author sings the praise of Joan of Arc, or of the modern French novelist; whether he brings in a financial measure or an Education Bill, his thought is uniformly perspicuous and his language invariably felicitous. But, paradoxical though it may appear, the chief merit of those three volumes to the outside reader lies in their total lack of originality. For if M. Poincaré's essays and speeches did reveal any striking originality they would only reflect the personality of the writer. On the contrary, being entirely devoid of originality, they express all the more faithfully the opinions of millions of Frenchmen. And for the first citizen of a democracy it is so much more important to be the spokesman of millions of his fellow-citizens than to merely express his own vision of the world.

III

A perfect equipoise of judgment, an instinct for realities, a sense of measure, what the French call " le juste milieu," and what Matthew Arnold would have called " sweetness and light," are amongst the most obvious qualities of Poincaré's writings. He is a man of principle; he is not a mere opportunist and a time-server.

" The foundation of all politics is ethical.

Politics are founded on a belief in goodness, in justice, in the love of truth, in the respect of human conscience, in the destinies of our country. Politics which are worthy of the name cannot live from day to day on empirical measures and contradictory expedients."

At the same time he is not a man of Utopias.

" The French people have faith in principles. They believe in the ideal. They have an innate taste and a traditional need for general ideas, but they do not confuse general ideas with vague ideas, principles with formulas, ideals with vacant vocables. They want solid living realities."

He is a genuine democrat. But he is also a resolute anti-socialist. He believes in the French Revolution, but he stops at 1789; he does not go as far as 1793. He does not think that the Republic can be saved by a Reign of Terror.

" With the party of agitation, of violence, of disorder, no political understanding is possible. A Government which would seek it would abdicate its authority, and would itself defy the law. A Government which would submit to it, or which would not repudiate it, would be swept away by its own hypocritical and equivocal policy."

He believes in the supremacy of individual

RAYMOND POINCARÉ, NATUS 1860.

reason and conscience. He is determined to resist the tyranny of the Church. But he is no less determined to resist the tyranny of the State.

" The action of Government cannot extend to the intimate thoughts of individuals. Political life is not the final end of Man. Human energies which put in motion the social mechanism are not entirely absorbed by it. The State cannot be allowed to encroach on the liberty of human reason, and this liberty outside the sphere of the State constitutes the inner life of the Soul. Our individual energies are not wholly attracted and captured by the social mechanism. Human Society is made of free volitions, and it is only on an absolute respect for human dignity that the greatness of a community can be established."

IV

It would be unfair to call Monsieur Poincaré a Conservative, and it is an appellation which his supporters would particularly resent, for the word " Conservative " is in very bad odour in France, and is synonymous with reaction. He delights in appearing as a Modern of the Moderns. He glorifies recent tendencies in Literature and Art. Yet his sympathies are with the past as much as with the present. He likes to repeat the famous words of Comte, " The Dead count for as much as the Living " (" L'humanité se compose de plus de morts que de vivants "). He has been nourished on the humanities, and he would probably contend that, even so far as the French Revolution is concerned, it was not merely an overthrowal of the past, but a return to the most ancient democratic traditions of humanity.

But the dominant note of Poincaré's Essays and Speeches is the patriotic note. He is a citizen of Lorraine, and Lorraine inspires her children with a patriotism more intimate, more anxious, more tender, than any other region in France. The love of France is his supreme inspiration. He is, no doubt, a good European, because he assumes that a good Frenchman must necessarily be a good European, because French culture is bound up with universal human culture. But I suspect that M. Poincaré has little interest in European culture as distinct from French culture.

V

This cursory analysis of the characteristics underlying M. Poincaré's writings will enable us to some extent to forecast the policy which the new President will try to impress upon his Ministers.

I do not think that his Home Policy will be one mainly of Social Reform. It will mainly be a policy of Republican concentration and of resistance to lawlessness.

Even as his Home Policy will be mainly a policy of resistance to the party of disorder, M. Poincaré's Foreign Policy will be mainly a policy of resistance to the encroachments of Germany. We may expect a firm though conciliatory attitude in international affairs, and a strict adherence of France to the Triple Entente. And this vigorous Foreign Policy will entail increased Naval and Military expenditure. That is another reason why his Home Policy cannot be one of Social Reform. Social Reforms cost a great deal of money, and for the next seven years all the available resources of France will be claimed by the exigencies of national defence.

THE NEW FRANCE

THE NEW FRANCE[1]

NOT many years ago, it was a fashion with superficial journalists and political philistines to speak of the decadence of the French people. Those were the days when our attention was perpetually being called to Sedan and Fashoda, to the crushing defeats and humiliations suffered in war and diplomacy, to the prevalence of religious strife and internal dissensions, to the Panama and Dreyfus scandals, to the decrease of the birth-rate and the increase of crime. It was a foregone conclusion that the doom of the foremost of the Latin races was sealed, and that the immediate future belonged to the Teuton.

I

As a matter of fact, the immediate future gave the lie to those prophecies. The prophets were

---

[1] I have included this Essay on the French Renascence, written three years ago, although it treats of the same subject as the more elaborate Introduction to the volume. But even though the sentiments and spirit of the arguments are the same, the Essays were written under entirely different circumstances and from an entirely different point of view. And the splendid fact of the French Renascence can bear repeating and emphasizing.

entirely misreading the phenomena of French life. They failed to see that it is a good sign, and not a bad sign, when a whole nation is convulsed when there is one miscarriage of justice, as in the case of the Dreyfus affair. They failed to see that it is a good sign, and not a bad sign, when a nation is so truthful that she must always lay bare her evils for all the world to see—as in the case of the Panama scandal. They failed to see that it is a good symptom, and not a bad symptom, when a nation is so passionately interested in religious truth as to be ever ready to fight for it. They failed to see that even civil strife is not necessarily a symptom of disease, but may, on the contrary, be a symptom of health. Only those nations know nothing of civil strife who always submit in passive and servile obedience to despotism.

And therefore what the prophets mistook for French decadence was nothing but a crisis of growth, antecedent to a rejuvenescence and a renascence of the French people. That crisis of growth might indeed produce a temporary weakening, as every such crisis does, but the French people did emerge from that weakening with that marvellous recuperative power and with that mercurial temperament which has characterized them through history. And, the crisis past, they once more appeared in the van of civilization, they once more astonished the world by the exuberance of their vitality.

II

Considering first the material prosperity of contemporary France, even those realists who take wealth as the chief criterion of national greatness must admit that in the abundance of her national resources France is at least the equal of any other Continental nation. There is no other nation which possesses so much accumulated capital. There is little pauperism in the big cities, and outside those cities there is little poverty. Amongst no other Continental people is wealth more evenly distributed than among that nation of peasant proprietors. Paris remains one of the two or three money markets of the world. Most of the great enterprises of modern times, from the Suez and Panama Canals to the Trans-Siberian Railway, have been launched with the assistance of French loans. Even Germany has again and again been compelled to appeal to France to finance her Imperial schemes.

III

If we pass from the consideration of the material prosperity of France to that of her political power, we find that here also she has been restored to a front place in the councils of Europe. After 1870, France knew a few years of international isolation and of diplomatic impotence. To-day France stands conscious of her strength, and opposes a united front to her enemies. But her patriotism has ceased to be aggressive; it is restrained and dignified. She still remains, even as all the world actually does remain, under the magic spell of Napoleon's personality, but she has ceased to glorify the pomp and circumstance of war. And her political power to-day is asserted as it never was before, in the cause of peaceful progress. England has understood the true significance of French power, and it is because she has understood it that she has entered into an " Entente Cordiale " with her neighbour. English statesmanship realizes that France is the key-stone of Continental Europe, that she holds the balance of power, that any serious blow aimed at France would be indirectly aimed at England and at European civilization, and that if it ever came to a European conflict, the decisive battles of

England would have to be fought, not against France, as in the past, but in alliance with France and on French battlefields.[1]

IV

It has often been found that material prosperity and political power deaden, for the time being, the spiritual activities of a people. This cannot be said of contemporary France, and her spiritual activities reveal no less the vitality of the race than her economic activities.

There are still to be found a few bigots who are fond of repeating that the French are essentially a non-religious people, a frivolous, light-hearted people, a sceptical people. Fifty years ago, Elizabeth Browning gave an answer to that calumny in an inspired passage of "Aurora Leigh":—

> "And so I am strong to love this noble France,
> This poet of the nations, who dreams on,
>
> . . . . . Heroic dreams!
> Sublime, to dream so: natural, to wake:
>
> May God save France."

In those noble lines, Mrs. Browning perceived the deeper truth, and read the French character

[1] Written in 1912.

with the intuition of poetic genius. If religion means essentially a belief in a Divine Purpose of humanity, if it means a belief in lofty ideals, if it means the fervid enthusiasm which sacrifices everything on the altar of those ideals, then there are no more religious people than the French. They are incurable idealists. From the days of Joan of Arc to those of Rousseau, the French have always been a nation of apostles and of propagandists, and they have often shown the intolerance and fanaticism of the true apostle. Most French wars have been wars of religion; they have been crusades for the triumph of a principle. Some of the most decisive political and spiritual revolutions in modern history have their source on French soil. And what is true of the past is true of the present. At least three great contemporary constructive movements are French in origin: that momentous struggle for spiritual freedom within the Roman Catholic Church which goes under the misleading name of "Modernism"; that far-reaching attempt at reconciling science and religion which is miscalled Pragmatism; and that portentous political philosophy of Syndicalism which is rapidly spreading all over Europe. Loisy, the father of "Modernism," Bergson, the father of Pragmatism, Georges Sorel, the father of Syndicalism, are all Frenchmen, and around those pioneers are gathered a host of seekers after the Truth.

V

Even the most severe critics of French culture have always admitted the supreme quality of the French intellect—its lucidity, its versatility, its ingenuity, and, above all, its intellectual honesty and integrity. It was therefore to be expected that a French revival which revealed itself so strikingly in the province of politics and religion, in an outburst of patriotic fervour and spiritual idealism, should equally assert itself in science, art, and literature.

In theoretical science the French have always retained their prominence. In mathematics, the purest of all the sciences, they can still boast of their traditional supremacy. I need only refer to such names as Poincaré. In the applied sciences, where they have often lagged behind the English, they have been the pioneers in the two new developments which are transforming contemporary life : the motor car and the aeroplane. Both have been from the first pre-eminently French industries. And in this connection we may apply to the French people in a modified form a famous epigram of the poet Heine: whereas the English may claim the supremacy of the sea, whereas the Germans may claim the supremacy of the land—to the French belongs the conquest of the air.

VI

But it is especially in the province of literature and fine art that the French Renascence has achieved its most signal triumphs. The French school of painting continues to draw its disciples from all parts of the world. In sculpture, Rodin is a giant towering above his contemporaries in splendid isolation. In literature there may be greater names than those of Anatole France and Maeterlinck, than Romain Rolland and Rostand; but certainly there are no names which are more universal.

VII

I have just mentioned the poet of "Chantecler." Some critics have wondered at the extraordinary popularity of Rostand's drama. But the reason is an obvious one. "Chantecler" has struck the European imagination because it is the significant symbol of the Gallic genius. "Chantecler" is the bird whose clear song ("le chant clair") heralds the light of day and the joy of life. Such has been for centuries the mission of France : to herald the dawn, to dispel darkness and reaction, to announce the message of a fuller life, a life more joyous, more bountiful, more beautiful.

And there also lies the real explanation of the universality of the French language. I have travelled in every country of Europe, of Northern Africa, and of the Near East. Everywhere outside the Germanic countries I have found French spoken and read in preference to any other language, and often in preference to the mother-tongue. And the French language is everywhere read and spoken, not because it is more beautiful than other languages. Indeed, I believe that English and German are at least as beautiful as, and are often much more expressive and much more impressive than, the French language. The French language is universal because the French ideals which the French language proclaims are themselves universal, because they appeal to the whole of civilized humanity, because they partake of the eternal verities.

FUNDERBURG LIBRARY

MANCHESTER COLLEGE

920.044
Sa74f

DATE DUE

WITHDRAWN
from
Funderburg Library